T0059663

the little book of

self-healing

150+ Practices for
Healing Your Mind,
Body, and Soul

Nneka M. Okona

Adams Media
New York London Toronto Sydney New Delhi

To you.
To all those who need to heal.
May your healing—
and the journey to getting there
—be glorious.

A adams media

Adams Media
An Imprint of Simon & Schuster, Inc.
100 Technology Center Drive
Stoughton, Massachusetts 02072

First Adams Media hardcover edition
November 2021

ADAMS MEDIA and colophon are trademarks of
Simon & Schuster.

For information about special discounts for bulk
purchases, please contact Simon & Schuster
Special Sales at 1-866-506-1949 or
business@simonandschuster.com.

The Simon & Schuster Speakers Bureau can bring
authors to your live event. For more information
or to book an event contact the Simon & Schuster
Speakers Bureau at 1-866-248-3049 or visit our
website at www.simonspeakers.com.

Interior design by Erin Alexander and
Alaya Howard
Interior images © 123RF/rawpixel

Manufactured in the United States of America

2 2021

Library of Congress Cataloging-in-Publication Data
Names: Okona, Nneka M., author.
Title: The little book of self-healing /
Nneka M. Okona.
Description: Stoughton, MA:
Adams Media, 2021.
Identifiers: LCCN 2021032923 | ISBN
9781507216767 (hc) | ISBN 9781507216774
(ebook)
Subjects: LCSH: Mind and body. |
Self-care, Health.
Classification: LCC BF161 .O556 2021 | DDC
128/.2--dc23
LC record available at
https://lccn.loc.gov/2021032923

ISBN 978-1-5072-1676-7
ISBN 978-1-5072-1677-4 (ebook)

contents

mind 15

body 75

spirit 133

acknowledgments

I'll keep this short because I have but a few choice words. I thought I would have more to say, but I don't. While I wrote this book, I was processing a thoroughly traumatic period of life. It felt nearly impossible to focus on healing myself, let alone write about it. To center the writing I was doing, I turned to those who have always been beautiful examples of what healing can look like in action—other Black women. Truly, there is nothing more beautiful than existing in this skin that I am in as a Black woman and belonging to a legion of brilliant and creative women. I'm in awe of each of you, young and old, dead and alive. Our will to live despite a world that often doesn't want us here inspires me. We insist on still showing up.

Healing is not for the perfect—truthfully, none of us are. It's simply for those who have the courage to try to do it, even if they struggle through it immensely and it causes more pain. Even if they are repeatedly retraumatized in crawling toward some sort of salvation, a bit of a reprieve. That's the lesson here for me and what I hope is the main takeaway for you too. Healing can take a lifetime. And that's okay.

Thank you to my parents, Sallie and Chidi Okona; my sisters, Nnenna, Chinelo, and Chioma; my agent, Beth Marshea; and Sarah Doughty and Julia Jacques of Adams Media, who were so understanding, as I often needed more time to take care of myself as I wrote. And thank you to a host of friends who have stood in the gap as I fought to care for my own wounds while writing this book: Hala Abdallah, Marissa Evans, Evette Dionne, Britni Danielle, Julia Coney, Jackie Bryant, Francis Thompson, Shayla Martin, and countless others. Thank you for your kindness, for supporting me as I spoke my truth, and for not judging me as I healed in my own way. You all are love in action.

And thank *you* for reading this book and for trusting me to guide you through. I hope you heal over and over again. And I hope that healing is beautiful.

*introduction

Self-healing is a particular type of inner development. While healing is the practice of binding up a wound and beginning the path to restoration, self-healing is centering *yourself* in that process. Each day you intentionally focus on nurturing your mental, physical, or spiritual growth— those important elements that make you who you are. You take charge of what in your life needs to be restored and empower yourself to do the things you need to do to get to a place of healing.

The Little Book of Self-Healing is your guide to healing yourself. Organized by the three main sections of mind, body, and spirit, each chapter offers dozens of actionable ways to take the lead and move forward in your journey of self-healing. With this book as a tool, you'll be able to banish whatever obstacles may be keeping you from living the life of your dreams. You'll:

* Learn how to be kind to yourself
* Explore the benefits of herbal medicine

13

* Practice sitting with what you feel without judgment
* Befriend that wonderful, important person in your life: *you*
* And so much more

Through incorporating all parts of your being in the task of healing, you live and grow in authentic wholeness. You lean on everything you are in order to inspire the renewal that is to come.

Take heart. The path of self-healing is a fluid, ever-shifting one. Just as there will be peaks, where you feel ready to take on whatever comes your way, there may also be valleys, where you feel doubtful about your abilities or compare your progress with where you think you "should" be. This is all normal. At every point along the way, remember that you are enough—regardless of where you are in your healing journey. Because it is *your* journey. You deserve to take that next step, to grab the reins and seize whatever it is that you are wanting and needing in life. Turn the page to claim the power and potential within yourself!

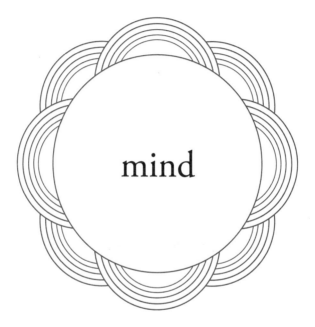

mind

Is there ever enough to be said about the power of the mind? Our minds have the ability to imagine worlds never seen before—and the power to keep us mired in what has threatened to break us and render us no longer whole. The mind also has a greater role in being a conduit of our self-healing. Through being cognizant that we possess the ability to facilitate growth and healing by working with, instead of against, our minds, we start to get somewhere—somewhere beautiful, uncharted, free.

In this chapter, you'll delve into activities that will help motivate and steer you toward healing your mental space. You'll become a student of your own healing by seeking out new resources, letting go of toxic positivity, calling to mind the joys in your life, and more. Self-healing starts with the decision to heal and being open to what comes as you do. Use this chapter to set off on your journey of healing with a focused, effective mental state.

Create a Reading List

❀

Sometimes in order to make the process of healing less daunting, we need to learn. The knowledge we uncover will enlighten us along on our way. Your path to healing will be unique, but you can gain insight from practices that have worked so well for others. Gathering books and other resources—pamphlets, old journals, magazine articles, and encyclopedia entries focused on healing—can be a good start in your own healing journey.

Of course, intentional reading needs structure in order to not become another source of stress, and reading lists are effective in this endeavor. To create a reading list, gather the titles of the books, articles, and other resources you've found on healing and organize them in a way that makes sense. Organization streamlines your reading and makes it easy to keep track of. Choose a method that feels intuitive—you might arrange them by main themes, resource length, resource type, or any other method you choose. Next, come up with a realistic time frame for reading each item on your list. For instance, for longer resources such as books, give yourself a full month to read, splitting up your study into weekly goals of a number of chapters or pages. Setting a time frame will help you stay accountable to your list.

Discern Trusted Sources

✺

When you search for wisdom in order to grow, change, develop, or heal, you may find yourself overwhelmed with competing voices calling out to you—advice from professionals online, notes from a trusted therapist, or suggestions from close friends and family. The question then becomes, "How do you know whether or not to trust the information you're hearing?" Discernment is the key. Ask yourself if the information feels right for you on an intuitive level. It is also beneficial to approach everything with a healthy amount of skepticism versus automatically accepting something as true.

Beyond these discerning tools, use research to quantify information you come across. If something seems like a stretch or wishful thinking, assume it is. If a certain name keeps coming up as an expert on a particular topic, dig deeper to find out if this person can be trusted. Have they done any questionable things or been connected to scams or scandals? What are their professional qualifications? What about personal experiences with that topic? Keep looking for boundaries to ground your research into healing.

Opt for Certification or Other Continued Education

✿

Sometimes what you read will not be enough. You may find the depth of information on certain aspects of healing to be more surface level or one-dimensional than you are looking for. Or perhaps the information is buried in terminology and concepts you are confused about. In those times, you'll have to dig in deeper. When reading books, listening to lectures, or delving into your own disciplined self-study proves to be lacking, obtaining certification or further education can make the difference. For instance, there are certificate programs in healing practices such as breathwork, meditation, and Reiki. Be sure again to verify credentials and listen to your gut when choosing a certification, class, or other program to pursue.

Look up the teachers leading these programs, particularly those that require months of commitment and/or a fee. Ask for details about accreditation and, if possible, talk to former or current students of the program to aid in your decision-making process.

Become a Student of
Your Own Healing

❁

Schooling is ruled by standards, convention, and tradition. These standards can facilitate important growth, but they can also feel limiting. Conventional schooling may present issues in black and white, making it difficult to think outside of the box. However, being a student of your own mental healing—and the transformation that follows—can be freeing. It can allow you to learn and digest information at your own pace—information tailored to what *you* need.

Being a student of your own healing means you get to make the rules to facilitate exactly what you are seeking in your healing journey. Jump-start this mindset by choosing to step into empowerment and shake off powerlessness. Write down objectives for yourself, similar to a syllabus a teacher gives you the first day of class. Come up with activities, readings, research, videos, or other lessons you want to incorporate into your learning process. You can use this book as a part of your self-syllabus. Make a schedule for your education. You might dedicate fifteen minutes each day to completing an activity in this book. Or allot a full afternoon one weekend day to researching books on healing and ordering a few that stand out.

Cultivate an Independent Study Group

✻

You don't have to heal alone. Instead, you can choose to bring others along in the journey with you as you discover more, unlearn old habits, examine your past trauma, and work to unpack all that has made its home within your mind.

One way to make this a shared experience is by creating a study group. Don't think of it as being like your old high school study group; achievement is not the point. The goal is to read thought-provoking books and passages together, share insight, and hold space for one another to witness growth and setback, and provide comfort for whatever hardships may arise. Study groups can be a soft place to land as you do the work of lightening your mental load.

When forming a study group, be discerning. Choose companions who are actively committed to doing healing work in their own lives and who have support systems already in place. This will help you remain motivated when things feel difficult. Set clear boundaries and make sure everyone understands that these gatherings are not therapy sessions. Be clear on the aims of the group so you all can thrive.

Prioritize Mental Health

❀

In the same way most of us recognize when our bodies are in need of a doctor's attention, we can tune in to the needs of our mental health and seek any necessary support. Mental health includes everything that goes into cerebral acuity, function, and overall resolve of our mind. Sometimes due to factors not in our control, we experience reduced mental health. Many people dismiss those needs that are less tangible than a physical ailment. But if ignored, poor mental health has the ability to derail many aspects of life. It can impact interpersonal relationships and the way we view ourselves, make it more challenging to complete tasks at work and in the home, and replace any motivation or interest with a heavy sense of hopelessness. Mental health is an integral part of your holistic health and elemental in embracing healing of any kind.

A few steps to take to prioritize your mental health and thus your healing include: using a mood tracker to notice patterns, using lists that help jog your memory and keep you on track with daily tasks, integrating mental self-care routines into your schedule, checking in regularly with your mental healthcare professional(s), and embracing trial and error to find what works for your unique mental health needs.

Let Go of Victim Mentality

❀

Those hard life experiences—the ones that shatter you, traumatize you, harden you—are real. The harm you have faced is real. The pain you've felt in the aftershocks of trying to piece your life back together and heal is real too. But you are not these experiences. You are much more than what has tried to break you and make you lose hope. You are the amazing things you've accomplished, and the things you will accomplish in the future. You are the friendships you have forged, and the moments you aided someone else. You are every trait—every habit and skill and interest—that creates the unique picture of who you are.

Let go of defining yourself by what has happened to you. Call yourself a survivor whenever you catch yourself starting to slink away from life in defeat—when you are tempted to wallow in what has gone wrong or may go wrong in the future. Repeat it to yourself as many times as necessary. You are a survivor, not a victim. Each thing that has occurred, whether difficult or devastating, you have survived. Surviving is what you do and what you were created to do. Be proud and move forward in healing.

Pursue an Integrated Life

❦

Boxes—boxes containing different things, different elements of who we are. This is what most of us do to try to make life more manageable: compartmentalize. We try to create discrete borders between the aspects of our lives: our close interpersonal relationships, career, spiritual community, and so on. But juggling jagged segments of ourselves can be exhausting, because we're not operating at our fullest capacity in all parts of our lives. Rather, we are bringing smaller pieces of ourselves to each experience. So why not merge all those elements of your world into an integrated life?

Psychologist, author, and motivational speaker Dr. Todd Hall identifies four steps you can take to live a less fragmented existence. First, identify your "theme" (what drives you in life). Second, evaluate how the puzzle pieces of your life fit around this theme. Third, tinker with those puzzle pieces until your life starts to feel less fragmented and more whole. Four, evaluate what feels missing from the picture.

To begin this process, call to mind your core values—the things that are most important to you. These may include things like family, honesty, compassion, friendship, and more. Naming these important elements can help you identify what drives you. As you name your values, consider what common theme(s) appear across them.

Envision a Love Space

❀

Every human on this planet wants to be accepted. We want to be loved, adored, cherished. And we want our minds to be respected and valued for the important, unique vessels that they are when we treat them with care.

Healing can be a lot of things. Terror and rage. Cyclical and nonsensical. We can go back and forth—up and down—between different emotions, thoughts, and beliefs. Eventually, we start to venture to somewhere sacred, and our healing becomes known to us in concrete, tangible ways. Wrapping our hands around it and tasting it on our tongues becomes less abstract.

At this point, you've made it: You've found your love space, where you can both accept and understand your healing. What does your love space look like? How does it feel? What does your love space allow within its presence? Maybe it's serenity, so you can feel able to heal. Or it takes the form of silence, so you can hear yourself think as you move through life and its many situations. Whatever the case, claim your love space as yours. Take it with you as you continue to heal. Envision it when you need to feel mentally clear and not bogged down with cerebral clutter.

Go Easy on Yourself

❄

Imagine you've made a mistake. Maybe you said the wrong thing to someone you care about and unintentionally hurt their feelings. Or perhaps while on your healing journey you slid back into an old habit that feels comfortable and familiar but that won't help you get closer to healing. You are a human being; you have a propensity for making mistakes. So even if you *have* made a mistake (or interpret a situation as a "mistake" on your part), it doesn't mean that you need to berate yourself and roll out the punishment for what you feel you deserve. No one deserves to be punished for showing up as infinitely human—you included.

The next time you feel tempted to beat up on yourself for making a mistake, try a few healing activities instead. Begin by saying kind things to yourself in a soothing tone, with reassurance that you are okay and that all will be okay. Then, take a few deep breaths to de-escalate your emotional state into one of calm. The world will not end because you are imperfect. Nor are you unable to heal because you are imperfect. Healing is a journey; along the way you're sure to stumble a time or two, and that is okay.

Stop Rumination in Its Tracks

❊

Cyclical, repetitive thoughts. Thoughts that keep us in a chokehold, rehearsing outcomes that often never come to pass. Rumination, as it is called, can be seductive. It presents itself as helpful—a way to control things outside of ourselves. Yet, in tunneling down a never-ending spiral of thoughts, we use up good, productive time and energy for something that ultimately leads to nothing but anxiety and grief.

To beat rumination requires a little practice. When you notice yourself slipping into rumination, when the thoughts become obsessive and repetitive, ground yourself in that awareness. Notice the thoughts sprouting in your mind, but before they bloom, delicately divert your mental attention to something else. It can help to choose an alternate thing to think about or to begin a task that requires your full attention. Each time you feel rumination starting to build, practice this routine of awareness and diversion. Over time, you'll become more adept at noticing when damaging thoughts begin, and you can delicately put them aside.

Say No to Toxic Positivity

❁

There's nothing wrong with choosing to see the good in things. Seeing silver linings, reframing things positively when faced with a less-than-sunny circumstance can feel like a practice in growth. However, living and healing with positivity that feels very black and white without room for any shades of gray can be limiting. Reframing sometimes erases or hides what may be hard or unwanted but important to healing.

When you feel compelled to offer up toxic positivity—painting what is sad, horrifying, and tragic in a positive light—refrain. Pause and consider whether this will be truly helpful to the person in question. If that someone is you, give yourself the space to process what has happened and hold the truth of it with you. Healing is a practice in radical honesty; give yourself and others the chance to move through the land of what is real and painful. When we face the hard parts in our lives, we build resilience that will be helpful as we continue to face the unexpected situations that life sends our way. There is no need to set off on a quest looking for the good when there is none to be found.

Remember Your Growth

❀

When you get to a certain point in your healing, when life takes you from a valley to a mountain peak, you will feel as if you should only be looking forward toward a brighter future. No longer should you look back into the heaviness of the past. But you should look back, and look back often. Look back as if your future healing depends on it. Because, to a certain extent, it does. The only way to appreciate the gifts that the past holds is to take the time to pause and look back on the footsteps that have led you to where you are. You can look to what you have already triumphed over as proof of what you are made of.

Write about your growth up to the present. Keep a running list of the moments of growth you are proud of that you can add to periodically. Or create a timeline of your life and add short descriptions of challenging moments that you overcame and were able to extract lessons from. Remember: You have survived everything that has come your way so far. Celebrate that.

Call to Mind Joy

❊

Joy does not hide. Unlike toddlers ducking behind doors or underneath beds in a game of hide-and-seek, joy is not waiting to be found, seen, and claimed. Joy is a force that can readily be accepted, embodied, and harnessed as a tool of healing. Joy is concerned with healing. Joy—shifting our mindset to embrace the good—is a practice in having faith that we can be happy. It also reminds us that there is levity to be found, despite the hardships we may be facing.

Joy is not selfish. Choosing joy is not an exercise in shrugging off the hard things, the heavy things, the sad things. Centering joy in your life and in your healing does not mean you ignore the ills of what it means to be human. It simply means that you are reserving a space to revel in the wonderful parts of being alive.

Call joy to mind regularly. Ask yourself in the morning what one thing you can do today to be in touch with your joy. Think of things that make you joyful or moments when you felt most joyous. Take yourself back to those experiences. If calling it to mind organically proves to be a challenge, schedule reminders or events in your phone.

Create Mental Space Just for You

❧

A maze of thinking, processing, and considering—our minds are the base of what it means to be human. Life happens and our mind shifts into gear, trying to find meaning in it, trying to discern the bigger lessons or truths, if any are to be found. Because of this, our minds can often be a noisy place of jumbled ideas, memories, worries, and more. Consider how healing the mind could clear a mental space that is reserved just for you.

Imagine an oasis away from the rest of the world. A space where you are not dedicating time to considering the feelings and thoughts of others, not thinking through how you will take action in complex situations, not trying to understand the past. A space where you can check in with yourself, your needs, and your wants. Where you can ponder whether you feel fulfilled or neglected. Where you can daydream about your biggest desires. Where you can reflect without judgment or consideration for anyone or anything beyond yourself. We all deserve that. *You* deserve that. Create a mental space for you. Designate days or times to regularly visit this space.

Manage Your Mental Energy

❦

Healing is an involved process. It takes mental energy—often a lot of it. It is important to manage your energy along the way.

What does it mean to manage mental energy? Notice what things cause mental drain (what leaves you feeling depleted). Notice when you are feeling mentally stuck (unable to reason or come to a solution for a sticky situation). Notice what time of day your mental acuity is at its sharpest and clearest, and when getting anything done that requires mental power becomes a drag. Being a witness to your mind is the first step to pinpointing what needs to be shifted.

Once you've identified imbalances in your mental energy, you can make a few concrete changes to help avoid burnout. For example, reserve tasks that require more mental energy to the time of day when you are most alert. You can also make the decision to divest from those tasks that only serve to deplete you. Managing your mental energy is like a puzzle. You shift things, remove pieces, or start the puzzle over if things don't fit. Use trial and error until you feel more mentally balanced instead of constantly exhausted.

Think Healing Thoughts

❊

What we tell ourselves absolutely exerts power. And being the keepers of our thoughts, we hold this power. We are able to stand at the head of our own lives and will our thoughts to be more uplifting—more healing.

One way to think healing thoughts is to use affirmations. Affirmations are uplifting words or phrases repeated with intention. Phrases as simple as, "My healing and wholeness are already mine" or "What I think, I will into powerful being" are examples of healing affirmations.

In using affirmations, you can interrupt unhelpful ruminations, cognitive distortions, and other negative mental habits before they bloom. You stop them when they are still seeds—little germinations of heady consequence. Find affirmations online that resonate with you or create your own. Watch how those words sow better seeds in your mind, and how they bear a bountiful harvest of healing.

Try Alternative Therapy Modalities

❀

Counseling and therapy are wonderful tools for healing. Meeting with a licensed professional whom you trust to walk alongside you as you heal can be tremendously effective. But there is more than one kind of therapy.

In Western medicine, the most common type of therapy is cognitive behavioral therapy (CBT). This type of therapy prioritizes shifting cognitive distortions and changing behavior to support healing. In a safe, trusting therapeutic relationship, the client feels encouraged in their journey.

Aside from CBT, the American Psychological Association advocates psychoanalysis/psychodynamic therapies, humanistic therapies (Gestalt and existential therapy are some examples), and integrative therapies as less common possibilities. Like CBT, these modalities incorporate talking to work through past trauma, but use other approaches such as mindfulness and supported action to meet that goal as well.

Depending on your mental health needs, certain therapy techniques will resonate more. As always, do your research. Consider your mental health needs and reach out to those who can answer questions to help you determine the best approach.

Look to Art

❖

One approach to healing and mental health is more creative than the common paths you may first think of: art. The premise of art therapy is that creative expression can act as a facilitator of healing. According to the American Art Therapy Association, art therapy uses the process of making art to improve your well-being.

More specifically, creative expression has been shown to reduce stress, increase mental function, and allow for a healthy release of trauma. This makes it an effective means of healing and bringing balance to your mental state. Fall into the beauty of creation with art in any of its forms. You can create a physical art journal in a special notebook, draw, paint, color, sculpt—whatever speaks to you. Healing can include common, practical steps, but you can also inject creativity into the process.

Talk to Yourself Lovingly

❅

Your thoughts can be a roaring voice of critique, doubt, and worry. But they can also be a voice of love, affirmation, and encouragement. In the quest for self-healing, consider self-talk as a path to reclamation. You can opt to reclaim your thoughts and use them for self-cultivation and healing rather than for self-doubt and harsh judgment.

Talking to yourself lovingly can be an adjustment at first. Embrace this new practice: When you've had a difficult moment, lend yourself softness. Say the words you'd most appreciate hearing from a close friend or family member at that time. In time, this will feel less contrived and more natural.

If you've already had practice in providing loving, gentle, and compassionate self-talk, inject some new energy into your self-talk. Maybe you've repeated the same affirmations for a while. Change them up! Look at where you are in your healing; shift your self-talk to meet your current needs. Try new phrasing that speaks to how you need to be loved and cared for right now by the most important person of all—yourself.

Be Selfish

❀

Words mean things. Even if we don't like what meanings are built when words are paired together, honoring the significance of words is crucial—especially when talking about self-healing. *Selfish* is not the boogeyman hiding underneath our beds, a word to be feared, to avoid at all costs. Though the term may conjure up images of those who are not concerned in the least about anyone else, who hoard their time and resources to only benefit themselves, it can also mean something else—something essential to mental health and healing. *Selfish* can be centering your own needs, prioritizing them as they deserve to be prioritized.

In this time of healing, in this time of trying to unburden yourself from the wounds that have formed over time, be selfish. Before showing up to give support to others, check in with your own mental well-being. Do you have the capacity to actively listen, to be of support and to hold space for someone else? If the answer to this question is no, focus your attentions on replenishing that mental energy now. To do so is the opposite of being uncaring: It is recognizing your cup needs to be filled up to the brim in order to have resources to share with others.

Take Your Time

✿

Heed your self-healing enough and you'll likely come to a conclusion: It can take a lifetime. As we direct our minds to be healed and whole again, we see that it can stretch along a path toward an invisible end. This is why self-healing is called a journey and a process. Yet we can still feel like we need to hurry up and move on, hurry up and be "over this" already.

Try something different instead: Take your time.

Healing doesn't need to be fast to be useful, real, or a good use of energy and time. In those moments when you are tempted to compare your healing journey to someone else's or to feel frustrated from a temporary setback or detour along the way, remind yourself that you are on a very personal journey. There is no time limit to healing. And there's no certain pace you need to maintain. If you aim to live each day better than your last, you are headed in the right direction. You can take your time. Here is your grand permission to do just that.

Clear the Mental Muck

❀

Things accumulate over time: memories, words and advice that may have been unhelpful or upsetting, mental hang-ups that feel impossible to release. Self-healing requires clarity and focus to make your entire life a container able to hold both the glory and grief that healing entails. You deserve to clear the mental muck—the leftover residue from the past—in order to be present for your healing and the wonderful things to come.

To clear mental muck, find a ritual that feels cleansing for you. This may mean journaling in the morning or evening to release all that is clouding your mind. It may involve going to a trusted friend or licensed professional (like a therapist, counselor, or social worker) to clear your mind through sharing. Or a physically symbolic activity may work best—for example, writing down how you feel, then burning the paper or throwing it out into water to let it go.

As you focus on self-healing, creating the space for healing to enter is essential. Steadily and routinely clear the mental muck to make that space. Honor the work that goes into your healing and you are more likely to see long-term effects.

Build a Meditative Practice
That Works for You

❁

Anchored in Southeast Asian practice, the goal of meditation is the ability to sit in an uncluttered space where you can clearly monitor (but not try to control) your thoughts as they drift in and out of your mind. Meditation is more than that, however. It is a chance to ground yourself when the outside world rages and chaos abounds. Meditation is the ability to go within and find a safe space to breathe.

Meditative practices are not one-size-fits-all, however. Meditation has been prescribed as a healing balm for many, but it can and should be tailored to your specific needs.

You can cultivate a meditative space in many ways. You can pursue a traditional meditation practice focused on sitting with your feet on the ground and taking deep breaths. You can use a walking meditation or guided visualization routine. Even cooking can be meditative. Explore the different options and choose what works for you. When you feel yourself teetering into a state of overwhelm, find refuge in your meditative practice. Relish the calm. Bathe in the peace. Wrap your arms around the solace in this. Remember, it is always there waiting for you when you need it.

Embrace Mental Strength

✤

There is more than one way to be strong and more than one way to see yourself as embodying strength. When it comes to our physical bodies, it's relatively easy to see strength when we've bulked up and added extra muscle to our form. While strength training increases physical strength, it's the process of self-healing that builds mental strength. Though less tangible than physical strength, mental strength can be witnessed in how we approach what happens in our lives in our responses to joyful times *and* those times marked by hardship.

When we heal from something, we don't think of ourselves as now perfect. Healing isn't about perfect or imperfect. So we cannot measure our progress in this way. Instead, it can be seen in our mental growth—our ability to reframe situations, bounce back from challenges, and not let what intends to maim us exact so much damage. Mental strength is the essence of this. Notice when you are processing what life brings, and avoid sliding into pessimism. Notice when you can let yourself feel and also accept that your feelings are not fact.

Mental strength is concerned with wisdom. You build it through what you have survived and what you discover about yourself.

Look Toward Resilience

❖

Life can sometimes harden us if we're not careful. In a quest to accept what is hard, the knowledge that we possess the ability to thrive can be lost. It can slide from the crest of our attention and become buried beneath the weight of what we have dealt with and continue to deal with.

But gentle reminders of resilience are everywhere around you as you live and as you work toward and through your healing. Find them and hold them close. Perhaps a certain person in your life—a close friend, a neighbor, a dear colleague—can serve as this example for you; someone who embodies the ability to bounce back from whatever is presented to them, good or bad. Let them be a shining example of who you can be too. Call them to mind.

Call to mind examples in nature too—a caterpillar that, during the traumatic experience of metamorphosis, remains present for their undoing, and unfolds into something beautiful; plants that endure a drought and bloom when rain and moisture return once again. Look for that inspiration and know that there's a chance for you too—if you believe.

Create a Plan for Upheaval

❁

Not everything will go perfectly. In fact, we should realistically expect that at some point, especially when knee-deep in our healing journey, life will fall apart. Accepting this is not being negative but accepting the eternal balance of living. As we work toward healing, we can prepare for those difficult moments. We can create a plan that is filled with the nurturing that will remind us that we will be okay.

When creating a plan, think honestly about your self-care practices. What are you currently doing for yourself when you need to feel nurtured and reassured? What have you been doing for a while that may no longer feel effective? Is there something you can swap out or adjust? Something new you could try?

Also think about what systems you can establish that won't require a ton of ongoing maintenance. For instance, if your support system is a huge part of what gets you through hard times, communicate with them in advance about what you need to feel supported. Talk to them about what that support looks like for them, too, so they can feel nurtured in their own times of need. Think ahead during the times when you aren't in the midst of heartbreak or mental clutter or anger.

Make the Choice to Heal

❀

Carrying our wounds, living in spite of what has harmed us, is what makes us human. Seeing healing as a choice can be a part of our righteous and deserved humanity too.

Some of us carry our wounds as a means of identity. We have lived with them for a time—maybe most of our lives. They become such a part of us that they are comfortable, even safe. It's hard to separate who we know ourselves to be—and whom others know as us—from the pain that has come to define us. For this reason, self-healing can feel strange or uncomfortable. There's now an unknown to contend with, as we think about what lies outside of our pain. Who are we when not taking into account what we have to actively heal from? Because of this unknown, we may resist healing or doing self-healing work.

But you deserve to heal. You deserve to define yourself not just through your greatest pains but also your greatest joys. To make the decision to heal, to choose to weather through its ups and downs, create an affirmation for yourself to repeat. For example, your affirmation could be something like: "I am worthy, loved, and honorable enough to heal. I deserve that and so much more." Repeat it as often as necessary until you have accepted it to be true.

Stop Personalizing

❊

Taking things personally is common. It's natural to take the words or actions of someone else at face value and assume it's communicating something about us. We do not often know what other things may be impacting their behavior. But what if you aimed to choose a different path here? What if you freed up the mental space where you hold these heavy memories of what others have said or done?

In his book *The Four Agreements: A Practical Guide to Personal Freedom*, Don Miguel Ruiz defines one of the four important agreements to make with yourself as not taking anything personally. He writes that in most cases, the actions and words of others are a sum of their own projections, their lived realities, and how they see the world. It is very much about them, not you—despite how it may seem in the moment. You have to learn to hold space for how others navigate their world and not let it hinder your own journey.

The next time you feel tempted to take something personally and internalize it, acknowledge this urge, then choose to extend compassion to yourself instead. Remember that someone else's version of reality doesn't necessarily intersect with yours.

Reparent Yourself

Tending to the inner child can be a healing experience. In reaching back to foster a close, healthy relationship with that younger version of yourself, you will find a beautiful opportunity to "reparent" yourself.

Reparenting is the act of giving yourself what you most needed as you were growing up. It means teaching and nurturing your childhood self beyond what your original caregivers were able to provide. Some of us may have been parented with tough love when we needed more tenderness as we processed our various experiences. Others may not have been encouraged to express or talk through emotions and learned to repress them as they got older.

Now that you are an independent adult, as a part of your healing you can stake a claim in your development by giving yourself what you needed—and what you may still need. What is that for you? Reflect and ascertain the answers. And once you have those answers, commit to giving yourself at least one of those things every day. It could be as small as letting yourself color in the morning to start your day because you enjoyed it as a child, or watching that favorite cartoon when you need a mental break.

Silence Your Inner Critic

❀

The tone, the words, and the cadence varies, but we all have an inner critic. An inner critic may guide us into a spiral of shame and guilt when we've made a mistake. Or it may take things one step further and loudly berate us until we're overwhelmed with a sense of failure.

The truth is that your inner critic doesn't come out of nowhere. No one simply starts life talking to themselves in harsh tones. You take cues from how you've been parented and how you've been treated in interpersonal relationships, particularly relationships with authoritative figures such as teachers and doctors. You learn through indoctrination, through what is modeled to you from the moment you are born. Self-regard is taught before it can be fully owned and understood—before it can be a self-healing decision.

It's time to take the reins over your inner critic and silence that harsh voice as it arises. When you feel pushed by your inner critic, practice repeating this phrase: "Thank you for trying to protect me. Thank you for noticing when I'm close to being in touch with my grief, my shame, my issues of worth. I can take it from here." This process gives credit to what your inner critic is attempting to do—then, with gentle reassurance, takes back control.

Become Your Own Cheerleader

❄

Being cheered for loudly is an affirming and validating experience. In a world that can do so much to tear you down and cause you to doubt yourself, having someone root for you and encourage you when you feel doubtful can be healing. The comfort comes in having someone who fiercely believes in you. It can be edifying for self-esteem, enforcing a sense of worthiness you may struggle to accept.

You can take it a step further and learn to validate yourself. You weren't created to exist on an island by yourself, but all things in your life starts with you—including encouragement. You don't (and shouldn't) need to wait for others to cheer you on in every triumph.

Validating yourself can be done in a few ways. Celebrate and be excited for yourself, knowing what you've persevered, without waiting for someone else to cheer you on. This could be as simple as doing a victory dance when something amazing happens or fixing yourself a celebration dinner complete with a cake to commemorate a triumph. Become your own cheerleader and notice how healing it feels to know you can count on yourself to lift you up through challenges and victories!

Understand That You Are
Not Your Wounds

❀

Every person walking this world—existing, growing, changing, healing—has baggage. These are the things they avoid discussing because it's too painful, or they feel too vulnerable. They dare not share certain dark stories and knowledge unless the environment feels safe. Our "stuff" is what often urges us to heal ourselves and change our lives. We want to outgrow the things that have harmed us and that we feel embarrassed about.

Although there is honor in owning your healing, it's important to note that you are not your wounds. Again: You are not your wounds. Your struggles, hang-ups, and mistakes are mere brushstrokes in the masterpiece that is you. There's no need to wrap your self-knowledge around a few strokes of paint.

Know this. Hold this close. And when the shame builds, the guilt appears, the tough stuff rages in the background, repeat to yourself this mighty affirmation to ground you: "I am not my wounds. I am more. I am abundantly more."

Combat Memory Loss

❀

As you've learned previously in this book, building mental strength and resilience is a part of self-healing. Trauma can directly impact memory, significantly diminishing parts of what you remember. Painful experiences that are too heavy to carry are buried deep in your mind, where even you struggle to access it. It is a form of self-protection. Incorporating simple exercises to lessen the likelihood that your short-term and long-term memory are diminished as a result of trauma will be beneficial to your overall mental strength.

If you notice your memory waning or simply want to improve your mental reflexes further, try crossword puzzles, writing short lists and memorizing them, or quizzing yourself on adjectives or nouns that start with certain letters. There are also apps you can download on your phone to do mental exercises regularly. Set a notification to remind you to complete them. Great apps include Elevate and Lumosity. Both employ a number of games to help strengthen your mental processes. Boosting your brainpower doesn't have to be boring!

Bow to Temperance

❊

In tarot, the Temperance card is a Major Arcana card depicted in the classic Rider-Waite deck as a tall woman with angel wings.

When the Temperance card appears in a tarot reading, the traditional interpretation is to advise restraint. Think deeply before diving into anything—including what feels safe, comfortable, and automatic. Tarot reader and social worker Jessica Dore has another interpretation for this card: Notice when you default to black-and-white thinking. In order to protect ourselves, we judge situations as being either this or that, allowing us to feel some sort of safety and control in the midst of a scary, unexpected situation.

Life has gray areas. There will always be nuance and further context to rely on, no matter the situation. Trying to force everything into neat little boxes is exhausting, and it only makes it all the more difficult to accept when something cannot be defined in these simplistic terms. You end up fighting against the complexities of life that are beyond your control. In order to heal, you must choose to see the gray areas. When you notice your mind jumping to a black-and-white kind of thinking, remind yourself of the gray shades. Acknowledge that there may be a realm of other possibilities beyond your assumptions.

Be Particular about What You Give Mental Power

❊

You possess the power to control your own mind. You choose what to give mental space to and what thoughts you allow to resonate and swell.

Self-healing requires being more guarded. That doesn't mean you should close yourself off from the world, and it definitely doesn't mean you should guard yourself against anything you could possibly think. Rather, it means you should be choosy about what you give a lot of mental space. Certain things—painful memories, harmful self-criticisms—will burden this space with negative, exhausting energy. Happy memories and empowering thoughts can help your mental space feel more positive and ready to take on what comes your way.

To begin guarding what you give mental power, set a time limit for reflecting and nursing ruminating, repetitive thoughts. You are allowed to think about the hard things, but within a limit. Start with a longer period of time—say, a few hours. Over time, work to decrease that limit to what feels appropriate for you. By taking control over what you allow to take up mental space, you demonstrate ultimate domain over your healing. That is vital. That means you are sincere about healing yourself and changing your life.

Use Complaints As an Entryway

❀

The irony in life, and in self-healing, is that often what looks like a closed door is actually an entryway—a path to a new life. Most of us feel moved to complain about many things. We may share our dismay with others, but usually it's our internal dialogue that roars with the things we detest and feel powerless over. But if we're a little imaginative, we can see those complaints as an entryway of their own—a chance to set some new boundaries or make serious adjustments to facilitate healing.

Find yourself complaining a lot about something or someone? Nursing negative or resentful thoughts? Communicate your limits. Tell that person or situation what your needs clearly are. Turn that grievance into a pathway for getting what you need. For example, if a friend constantly calls you first thing in the morning and it throws off your entire day, directly tell them that morning calls don't work for you and suggest another time of day that does. Tell them if they call you in the morning you will not be available to answer. And if they continue to call in the morning, reinforce the boundary by not answering even if you are able to.

Set Goals for Your Healing Journey

❁

Setting out on a journey to self-healing can be overwhelming. There are ups and downs to endure. Goal setting can give you a sense of focus. By determining specific goals in your healing, you can sort through and organize your thoughts, feelings, and experiences, and create the path to what you seek.

First, spell out your specific healing goals. A goal might be to become more connected to your body through physical movement or to find a therapist. Set aside a dedicated time to create your goal list, and make the process fun. Invite in food, drinks, or music. These goals are your dreams for your future self. They are not things to dread, so get excited! Focus on the bigger goals and try to restrict your list to what feels most important now.

Next, give your goals realistic time parameters. Making a five-year plan may be too ambitious and discourage you before you even begin. Instead, break your goals down into small time increments that feel manageable: week by week, month by month, quarter by quarter. Break down the goal itself into small steps that can be completed in these time increments.

Try Hypnosis

❀

A more unique approach to self-healing, hypnosis has a wealth of power when it comes to moving people toward a deeper understanding of their own inner workings.

This is not hypnosis as you may initially think of it—those onstage acts put on for crowds to enjoy purely for laughs. This is the practice that has been used for decades to process trauma. It is a method that has helped clients make huge leaps in healing after several consecutive sessions. The goal of hypnosis is to put the client into a trance that allows for subtle suggestion to facilitate healing. For example, hypnotic suggestions can uncover painful memories that were blocked and had been holding the client back from healing. They can also guide the client through a trauma in a more intentional way that helps them notice things they may have overlooked. A hypnosis practitioner will generally create an atmosphere of calm and ask you to relax both prior and during your trance.

If hypnosis seems as though it could be helpful for you, find a reputable hypnotist to facilitate your sessions. The National Board for Certified Clinical Hypnotherapists is a great resource. Their website (www.natboard.com) lists practitioners' names and certifications. Try something new and you may be surprised by the healing that comes.

Laugh Your Way to Mental Ease

❊

Think about the last time you deeply laughed. The sound of the laughter echoing around you. Tears rolling down your cheeks as the laughs escaped your mouth. A tightening in your stomach as your muscles contracted. Laughter feels good, even if it lasts for just a moment.

If you're serious about your healing and loosening the grip that your past wounds have on you, you may be tempted to make your entire world about healing. While healing is certainly serious, laughter can help lighten its mental weight. It can help you relax and even see things from a new perspective.

For some mental ease along this often-heavy path to healing, try laughing in moments when you're stressed. Use corny jokes or call a friend with the request that you want to laugh. Watch a funny video or listen to an episode of a comedy podcast. Have the courage to take a breather and not take yourself so seriously all the time.

Give Yourself a Break

✺

Taking breaks is not merely a snappy jingle for the Kit Kat chocolate bar. Taking breaks is a key to resiliency and handling healing in way that doesn't become exhaustive.

Think of it this way: When you are working on any sort of project, you take breaks. These could include a break to use the restroom or to get a snack. Your break could involve checking in with your partner or children, your boss or parents. These breaks are included because it has been proven that when working steadily toward any sort of goal, taking breaks throughout allows you to come back to the task refreshed and ready to get more done. Look at giving yourself a mental break during your self-healing process too.

Set a reminder to prompt yourself to pause. Take this time as an opportunity to not worry about continued healing or try a new healing venture. Take a break and see yourself return to your healing ready for what lies ahead. Breaks are truly restorative.

Return to Your Breath

❊

Most of us know what it feels like to be completely over-whelmed and mentally wrung out. Thoughts no longer come easily, or the ones that do often veer into negativity and pessimism. Cognitive distortions abound. Automatic thinking and rumination reign supreme. In these moments, returning to your breath, especially when focused on bringing healing into your mental space, can be life changing. Deep breaths can de-escalate intense mental states and clear your mind of clutter.

Return to your breath by taking a moment to pause and breathe in through your nose. Hold the breath in for about five seconds, then breathe out deeply through your mouth, releasing the air from your stomach. Breathe your way through whatever arises until you feel a sense of calm.

Return to your breath often as a means of recentering and resetting your mind for more healing as you move forward.

Uncover Your Life Purpose

❖

Rick Warren's bestselling book *The Purpose Driven Life* lays out a framework for evaluating what you are here on this earth to do—your purpose. Finding this purpose can give you a direction that is healing. It eases that feeling of wandering aimlessly and being lost. It provides mental clarity and lights a fulfilling path.

Discovering your purpose is chiefly a process of self-inquiry and trial and error. To begin that journey, consider what you're most passionate about. Are there activities that you would do even if you weren't paid for them? What part of your passions could be put to work in service to others and improving the world around you? The answers to these questions are the key to living a life filled with purpose. Once you have identified your purpose, think of what steps could be taken to weave that purpose into your daily life.

Be Honest about Where You Are

❀

Dwelling in the land of delusion—refusing to see things as they truly are—can be crippling. In choosing not to be honest, we cost ourselves mental peace and we work in direct opposition to our self-healing. In order to heal we must get honest about what we need to heal *from*, even if it is unpleasant to think about.

Being honest about where you are in your healing journey may seem scary, but it makes the steps yet to be taken a little easier. In honesty, there's clarity that can help light your journey. Start your honesty practice by taking stock of how far you've come in your healing and how far that is from where you'd ultimately like to be. Remind yourself throughout this process that you are human—that all progress is progress, no matter how small it may seem. From there, pledge to keep going, even if you're far from achieving your primary goal, or you're close but feeling so weary you're tempted to give up. Remember that giving up is most alluring when you're closest to a breakthrough or a pivotal moment of transformation.

Honesty doesn't have to be forceful or loud. Your practice of honesty can be a time of quiet and compassionate acceptance of where you are. Let it be encouraging so that you are motivated to keep moving forward.

Be Honest with Others

❊

Thinking our truth can be instinctual. Speaking our truth, however, can be daunting, especially if being honest is a new practice, or you tend to try to please everyone. But honesty must be practiced regularly in order to facilitate healing. Through speaking up honestly, you avoid allowing emotions like hurt and anxiety and anger to fester and build within. Truthful communication helps you release these emotions in an effective way.

You can begin taking small steps to be honest with others. If speaking your truth feels scary or uncomfortable, communicate that to those who you'd like to be honest with. Start with people who make you feel comfortable and safe. Tell them your desire to honor what is on your mind. Ask them to hold you accountable and not let you shy away from the truth. Once this understanding has been put out there, you will be more motivated to start being honest. And others will be motivated to help you speak honestly. If you're already practiced in speaking your truth, reflect on anything you've left unsaid and pledge to express it.

Speak your truth to others. Be proud to let your honesty soar and sing so that others will know that you are being true to yourself. Most important, *you'll* know that you are being true to yourself.

Decide What Changes
Need to Be Made

❀

Change is revolutionary. When we move to change or adopt changes beyond our control, we are telling ourselves that change is healing, that it can renew what is broken and improve what is no longer helpful.

Deciding what changes need to be made for your mental healing and wholeness begins with simply noticing what could be different. This shouldn't require a lengthy internal interrogation. Most of us know what changes we need to make if we take a moment to consider them. They show up in what feels worn out, in what is habitually done but has lost its effectiveness. Make a mental list of these things. Don't hold anything back; be honest.

Then take action. See the changes that need to be made with piercing honesty and begin making them. For instance, you may find yourself struggling with poor mental focus and mental fatigue. A needed change might be a better bedtime routine, such as going to bed earlier and keeping technology out of the bedroom at night.

Set and Stick To Self-Boundaries

❖

Most boundary work is outward bound. It's focused on what is around us—our relationships to people, places, and things. Those who have become drained, resentful, or frustrated can set boundaries as a way of healing their mental state.

Boundaries can be a personal endeavor too. They can be used to peer into your inner life and notice where you are not heeding your own needs. This is what boundaries are truly about: knowing what you need, recognizing those needs, and working to ensure they're met.

To set (and stick to) boundaries with yourself, consider the areas of your life where you feel a lot of frustration. Are you cranky when it comes to certain elements of work? Plan to set a time limit to complete those tasks as soon as possible so you can move on to other, less irritating things. Is your hunger uncontrollable late at night and you often give into snacking? Set a hard limit for the last time you will eat, and drink water or decaffeinated green tea to ward off cravings. Instances like these are opportunities to listen to your limits and mold your life around them versus pretending they don't exist.

Develop Self-Trust

❧

Self-trust is a key to loosening the grip of past pains. It is knowing that you have your own back, even if no one else does. It's a crucial part of healing and mental wholeness. As life twists and turns, the one constant you have to lean on is yourself. This is your journey, regardless of who may travel along it with you at different points. You will need to be able to rely on yourself for strength, and trust that you know what is best for yourself.

To cultivate self-trust, consistently and routinely choose nourishing practices. These could involve doing brain exercises to reinforce neuroplasticity or committing to regular therapy appointments to regulate mental health. When you know that you can count on yourself to keep your own word and to care for yourself no matter what happens, your trust in yourself grows. This is what is needed to heal—consistency, steadiness, routines, rituals. All these nourish your mind and contribute to your being a fuller, whole, sincere person.

Let Go of What Was

❖

There's sentimentality and nostalgia attached to what we've always known. Those certainties create comfort in our minds. However, when learning to embrace healing, you'll need to diverge from mental patterns that aren't serving you. Let go of conclusions that may not be correct. And release the image of who you considered yourself to be in the past. By doing this, you can create space for what is to come: healing.

Letting go is grief work. You are losing something you held close. Make this process easier to bear by surrounding yourself with mental comforts. Repeat nourishing affirmations to yourself as comfortable reminders. Visualize letting go as releasing balloons into the sky and watching them float away into the clouds. Paint a picture of the balloons being different colors, if that would be helpful, and dedicate one color to each thing being released.

As painful as letting go can sometimes be, it is an integral part of healing from the past and shifting into new seasons. In order to let the newness float in, you are called to release what no longer serves you. Think about your balloons. And let the levity of that release inspire you to allow in everything that has been healed.

Hold the Grief

❀

Grief is a constancy. No matter how carefully you may navigate life, you will encounter loss, disappointment, hardship, even betrayal. Progressing through our healing, through the changes we must make and accept, introduces us to a grieving process too. When we heal, we are walking toward a new version of ourselves. And we are letting go of what we used to be. It is a good shift, but can also be a sad one. The you that you were previously in your journey is gone and will never exist again. This is a loss that should be properly mourned. Grief must be held, not ignored. When we hold our grief, we integrate it into our new lives after loss. And in doing so, we allow ourselves to accept our losses and heal from them.

Initiate holding grief by naming any impactful losses you've experienced along the path to healing. Plan a ritual for mourning those losses. Your ritual could include lighting a candle in memory of the losses, naming what they are, and giving yourself space to express whatever emotions arise.

Gently and honorably hold your grief for the past in order to fully accept what is no more. Then you can move forward with a lighter mind, making room for the changes to come. Holding your grief will ultimately help you heal.

Disarm Anxiety

❊

Anxiety lurks in unsuspecting places. And the force of anxiety has the power to control your mind, making efforts in self-healing that are rooted in mental presence an arduous task. There are, however, ways to disarm anxiety and take back its power.

Begin by identifying how anxiety plays into your experiences. What signs or symptoms of anxiety present themselves: racing heartbeat, sweaty palms, miscellaneous gastrointestinal issues, insomnia, lack of appetite, racing thoughts, persistence in panic unprompted by external stimuli? Which of these come up most often? Once you've uncovered how anxiety manifests for you, consider both professional support and self-coping mechanisms. Some anxiety coping mechanisms include practicing mindfulness, breathing deeply, and meditating. Depending on your experiences with anxiety and the recommendations of your healthcare professionals, anti-anxiety medication may also be helpful. It can bolster any coping strategies.

Don't let anxiety rule your mind and life as you heal. There are resources and sources of support to help you along your way.

Face Depression with Compassion

❈

There may come a time during self-healing that depression roots itself in your mind. Or you may find depression accompanying you throughout your journey in life. Depression presents in a multitude of ways, most commonly as sleeping very little or excessively; poor hygiene and grooming habits; and increased or decreased appetite. Some of the signs may overlap with common anxiety symptoms (see the Disarm Anxiety activity).

To face depression, notice what signs resonate and how often they arise. Do more research into depression as well to truly understand it and uncover coping strategies that help you. Talk to friends who may have had similar struggles. Look for a therapist if you determine that professional support may be beneficial for you.

Face this period of mental self-inquiry with as much compassion as possible. If you belong to a marginalized community or sit at the intersection of multiple marginalized identities, this nonjudgment is especially crucial. The stigma of mental illness can get in the way of recognizing struggles and finding ways to treat them.

Depression is not beyond help. Nor is it the end of the world. There is still life to be enjoyed and possibilities to be seized.

Explore Your Subconscious

❊

Imagine a massive iceberg. On the surface, the iceberg may look small, but in reality, what is visible is only a fraction of what lies beneath—far more ice, far more weight.

Our subconscious is like this. *Psychology Today* defines our subconscious as thoughts and realities that may not be consciously known to us. In order to fully heal our minds, we have to make friends with our subconscious and the messages it presents. When we become aware of the thoughts, feelings, and conditioning buried here we can begin to heal from what keeps us tied to the past, weighs us down in the present, and holds us back from a happy future.

Begin to understand your own subconscious by becoming acutely aware of your automatic thoughts. Each day for one week, spend some time writing down everything that pops into your head. Reflect on these thoughts and which ones may not be serving you well. Then, be willing to change those harmful messages. Acknowledge them when they come, then consider alternatives.

Be on guard, and in the future, use the knowledge of your subconscious to understand a more accurate mental reality. These hidden assumptions don't have to steer your life or your self-healing journey.

Become Solution-Oriented

❁

Pathways to our healing are right in front of us. When it comes to mental self-healing, as the journey progresses, we're pushed to think of solutions instead of dwelling on problems.

Solution-oriented outlooks can sometimes get a bad reputation for not allowing the person to be fully present with what is difficult or traumatic. It can be seen as concentrating too deeply on "fixing" the person as if they are broken—a project to be completed. But humans are not projects.

The true focus of the solution-oriented approach is being able to recognize *when* looking for a solution and facilitating mental repair is the best path to take. You'll know your situation calls for being solution-oriented if it has become a chronic issue in your life—one that comes up again and again, asking to be resolved. From there, you create a plan of attack. Are there people to be called on for assistance? Other resources to be tapped in to? Make notes and create a to-do list for solving the problem. Watch solutions create a feeling of accomplishment and peace as you spot issues, troubleshoot, and put new systems in place.

Honor the Connection Between the Mind and Heart

❀

Many believe that the mind and heart are endlessly competing for the spotlight—that either our mind is right *or* our heart is right. Some even refer to their struggles following their heart or listening to their mind as proof. But your mind and heart are equal forces within you, and each has wisdom to share.

To honor the mind-heart connection, learn how the two work in tandem. Recognize that you have never made a decision or reached a point of self-realization without engaging both parts. A potential move to a new city, whether or not to enter into a new relationship—big decisions need insight from your head *and* heart to determine what is right for you. Choose to actively engage your heart and mind together as you heal. Listen to what comes up for you mentally along the way, and bow to your heart's tenderness as well. If practicing this is new, ask friends or other trusted people to hold you accountable for this shift you're making in honor of healing.

There is no battle between the mind and heart. The two are different spheres rotating around each other in harmony. In order to realize true mental healing, accept this. And see the two as friends to be collaborated with often.

Debunk Automatic Thinking

❄

Like a Formula One race car driver, automatic thinking is fearless and self-assured. Watch out when automatic thinking is in the driver's seat—it has an agenda of its own. Especially if you're in the business of caring about your mind and its role in self-healing.

Automatic thinking are those thoughts you have that seem to pop into your head out of nowhere. Something happens, a word is said, a circumstance unfolds, and without allowing for any sort of deep introspection, you form an assumption or pass a judgment. When it comes to mental health and healing, automatic thinking robs us of the ability to examine the facts and make up our own minds with a clear head.

You have a few options to combat automatic thinking. One is to be willing to challenge what conclusions you arrive at. For instance, if something a friend said made you feel foolish, ask yourself why you raced straight to that assumption. Is this something you've been told about yourself before? Something you tell yourself? Then, be willing to suggest an alternative. You can also repeat an affirmation to help you challenge the assumptions, for example, "I am willing to see things differently. I am willing to hold space for other truths to exist."

Own Your Mind and Your Life

❀

Our beautiful minds—these gardens of brilliance, insight, witnessing, fact-finding, introspection, and reflection—are the ripe ground for healing our mental selves. When you own your mind, you own your healing.

Everything that is now, everything that you know about yourself to be true, is yours. You are yours too. You belong perfectly to you. To stand in this place of acceptance, practice acting as if your life truly does belong to you. Remind yourself when circumstances are hard and undesirable that you can trust yourself, that you are dependable, capable, and powerful. That even if you've never been through this before, you possess the ability to endure and get to the other side.

Then embody that through mental confidence. Think with authority and speak your truths with authority. Watch the mental roadblocks clear away before your eyes. It is possible if you start with owning your inner power. Are you willing to dwell in the abilities of your mind?

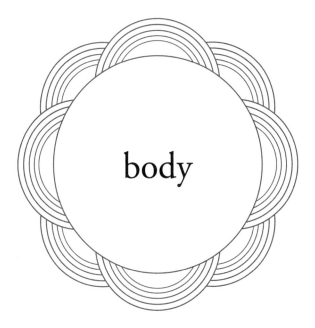

body

Writer and Black feminist Audre Lorde once said, "We have to study how to be tender with each other until it becomes habit." Though she was speaking about our interactions with others, it also fits for the care we give our own bodies. Just as we dedicate time and effort in treating others well, we should treat ourselves with the same level of care, regardless of whether it may feel less intrinsic to do so. In fact, it's only after we tend to our own needs that we can extend our energy to those around us.

In this chapter, you'll work on healing both your relationship to your body and your body itself. You'll drink a cup of tea as ritual, practice mindful eating, incorporate more nourishing cooking habits, and more. Formed over time and through consistency, habits take effort to change and maintain. The habitual process of being tender to your body, learning the wisdom it has to offer, and caring for it when it feels weary, is built as you heal. In this chapter, you'll uncover the tools to go onward in your self-healing and to mold this path in the way that feels right for you.

Sip Slowly to Healing

❊

A cup of tea starts with tea leaves. Whether these leaves are bundled into a tea bag packed in a box or are loose leaves ready to be packed into a strainer, the tea leaves themselves make all the difference. Choose a cheap, mass-produced brand, and your tea might taste flavorless and mediocre. Put loose leaves into a tea strainer or infuser that is old or unclean, and you could get the same effect.

But other factors also matter: the water temperature, how long the tea steeps, even the shape and depth of the mug it's served in. Don't skimp on the tea you choose or cut corners to get a quick finished cup. Put care and consideration into your choices. Note whether you're making a cup of green, black, or herbal tea, because water temperature and steeping times vary depending on these types. If you want it milky, add oat, almond, coconut, or cow's milk, half-and-half, heavy cream, or even condensed milk. And then, inhale the aroma, wrapping your hands around the warmth of your mug as the wisps of steam dance upward.

Take that first magical sip and relish the healing nourishment you've gifted your body with a beverage you concocted just for it.

Let Go of Hustle Mentality

❖

Most of us have been indoctrinated to value hard work and achievement above all else. Living in a capitalistic society reinforces this value, and if you belong to a marginalized community this idea may have been driven home even harder. It may have been an important value instilled by a parent or guardian. The hustle mentality is antithetical to letting us rest. Feeling like we need to relentlessly chase after the next thing or jump hurdle after hurdle to claim another achievement is not only exhausting but also burdensome. The chase, the grind, the pursuit of what is to come, robs us of presence, of connecting with others more deeply, and of connecting with ourselves.

The way to live and to heal is to release the need to hustle and to sacrifice to remain at the head of the pack. In this release, we can center our priorities on the things necessary to our wellness, such as giving our bodies the rest they need. Notice when you are forsaking rest to work beyond your limits. Talk yourself into taking that rest, that pause, regardless of the urge or pressure to skip it. Know that those tasks and to-dos will still be there if you put them down for a time. As a human, you need a reprieve now and then to be able to function at your best.

Practice Mindful Eating

❄️

The school of thought surrounding mindful eating is not a new phenomenon. Almost three decades ago, Evelyn Tribole, MS, RDN, and Elyse Reach, MS, RDN, penned a book that changed the landscape of nutrition and self-care forever. It was called *Intuitive Eating: A Revolutionary Anti-Diet Approach*. The book, created as a guide to help those searching for a different, happier relationship with food and their bodies, helps ease people into mindful, intuitive eating.

What is mindful eating? It focuses on tuning in to our bodies as we eat. No watching TV, no squeezing chores in between bites: Our complete attention is on the act of eating and thus shifting our relationship to food—and healing those knotty places to forge ahead in something new. Through mindful eating, we give our bodies the time and space they need to tell us when we are nourished, rather than racing through a meal so quickly and with so little awareness that we end up overly stuffed. We also bring joy in to the act of eating, and tune in to what not only *tastes* good but what *feels* good for our bodies. This can encourage more nourishing, healing food choices in the future.

To begin the journey of mindful eating, let it become a sacred, undisturbed activity with no distractions.

Prepare Your Kitchen for Healing

❀

It takes practice to change our relationship with food from one of convenience, frustration, or avoidance to one of self-care that contributes to healing from the inside out. It also takes a little structure to ensure you have a setup conducive to a successful cooking experience. To start, assess your cooking workspaces. Is there enough space for you to prepare meals? If not, consider purchasing shelving, a portable island, or other organizational tools to make more space. Are the necessary preparation spaces clean and clear? If not, tidy and sanitize them. Set the intention to always keep them clear and ready for cooking; view them as pieces of the sacred space that is the kitchen.

If you do this assessment mindfully, you'll set yourself up to go from being hungry to having a meal on the table in less time—with less stress.

Try Meditative Knife Skills

❊

Knives are used in the kitchen to prepare odds and ends: dicing, chopping, julienne slicing, mincing, snipping off edges and bad corners. For many who venture into the kitchen at their leisure, hoping to try a new recipe for lunch or dinner, knives are either a formality taken for granted or a source of intimidation—especially if you've never been taught how to properly wield them.

To fully connect to this powerful tool and soothe any nerves you may have in using it, position your knife with the tip resting on the cutting board and slowly rock it back and forth as you cut, creating a sustainable rhythm. Allow yourself to get in this groove and tune out any distractions—appropriately watching your workspace and being careful to avoid cutting fingers. See how soothing this activity can be when it is your sole focus. This is how chopping and dicing transition from the mundane to meditative—from a task of dread or annoyance to one where racing thoughts slip away and you focus on nourishing your body.

Recalibrate Your Concept of Rest

❃

When was the last time you fully rested? When you let the worries of your day fall to the wayside and focused on healing your body? When you took care to calm your nervous system by pausing from the stresses of life? If the answer is "never" or that you can't remember, that's okay. You, like many, are the product of a capitalist society that values productivity, even if it comes at great sacrifice to the body.

Just as we tend to other things that we rely on—our home, our physical appearance, our cars (lest they bottom out while driving)—we have to look at rest as being a necessary component of what it means to live. You can start this journey by paying attention to when your body speaks to you, and listening to its wisdom. Take a pause when your body says it is tired. And encourage all those you care about to tend to rest when they need it too.

Reorient to a Slower Pace of Life

❊

As the age-old children's story "The Tortoise and the Hare" demonstrates, slow and steady wins the race. But if most of us know this, why is slowing down to be more intentional in our lives such a battle? Because speed is praised. Speed is idolized. We are awarded for finishing jobs ahead of schedule. We are pressured to meet tighter and tighter deadlines.

But while it is often overlooked, slowness is a gift. Slowness is stopping to savor the sweetest moments of life. Slowness is being present for the joys and pains as they arise rather than dwelling on regrets or grievances of the past or anxieties about the future. A slower pace of life means you can pause long enough to see what truths come to you simply by virtue of limiting distractions and taking everything in.

To embrace a slower pace of life, recognize when you rush through situations, feelings, or moments. Ask yourself why you have an inclination to do so. For instance, if you rush past moments of high emotion, are you afraid that you'll never be able to escape a certain emotional state? Every habit serves a need. Getting clear on where your own tendencies to rush originate can aid your healing toward a more intentional, present life.

Be the Chef of Healing

❀

Cooking is a way to give your physical body the nourishment it needs to heal and thrive. Cooking can also be fun if you create the room for it to be a space of exploration and creativity rather than something you simply must do in order to survive. Creating a roster of delicious foods you can rely on time and time again and rotating them in and out each week is one way of making it easier and more enjoyable to cook regularly—and ensuring you like what ends up on your plate.

Building that stable of recipes requires self-inquiry and familiarizing yourself with the things you already like to eat. Are there certain forms of protein and grains that you find yourself gravitating to? Start a list of your favorites. From there, a theme should start to emerge. You'll see main dishes or sides that declare themselves. Leave room on your list for things that are aspirational as well: dishes you love ordering and eating from restaurants but have not tried or mastered yourself. If you'd love to conquer preparing any of these dishes, now is the time to practice! Cooking is an art form steadied and strengthened through trial and error until all the pieces magically come together.

Water Your Body

❄

From the beginning of our lives, we are told about the importance of water. Health classes in school pass this along in prescribing the standard eight glasses of water per day. We look to water to quench our thirst when we are dehydrated and give us energy throughout the day. Water replenishes and resets our bodies. Adequate amounts of water can lead to moisturized skin, more restful sleep, and the ability to better manage your appetite and ward off headaches and other body aches. And yet for some of us, making sure we drink enough can be a struggle.

If you've found drinking the proper amount of water each day to be an uphill battle, invest in a water bottle that you like and that is a convenient size to carry with you. Then start your new regimen slowly. Don't plan to drink a gallon of water today if you barely drank a glass yesterday. Set a realistic goal based on how much water you drink now and build on it over time.

Choose Lifestyle Changes
over Trends

❊

It is our birthright to feel good in our bodies. It is our birthright to find what works for us in this life in order to facilitate those good feelings. It is our birthright to make changes if how our bodies feel is out of alignment with who we know ourselves to be. Change is what we need—not fad diets that encourage negative feelings about our bodies.

Popular diets are appealing because they make the idea of reorienting ourselves to have a better relationship with our bodies seem easy. They promise a few steps to happiness rather than admitting the harsh truth that making long-term changes can be difficult and requires repeated effort. Changing ingrained habits is hard. Accept that choosing to do the next popular eating challenge that everyone else is doing won't be a sustainable practice. Admit that what you need is a more holistic, more healing, more befitting change than a one-size-fits-all "cure." Choose to go in the direction of that wholeness one step, one lifestyle change, one decision at a time.

Find Movement Activities
That Resonate

❊

Our bodies were created to move. Limbs, joints, and connective tissues bind together to enable fluidity and flexibility as we move from one place to the next. What movement activities we choose to take up for our health don't have to be punishment. You can choose activities that give you a burst of endorphins while also promoting healing. Everything is a choice.

Perhaps you're already an active person. Movement is something you do regularly either because you know you should or because an active lifestyle aligns with other goals. Perhaps you're not an active person. You don't exercise regularly because you dread it, or it feels like a challenge to fit it into your schedule. Either way, turn your focus to finding what resonates. Don't look at movement as yet another thing on your to-do list or as something that you simply must endure. You may have been conditioned to this attitude without your realizing it, but it can be shifted. Try out different kinds of movement and pay attention to what feels good and whether you feel drained or revitalized after doing it. If you feel good, if there is no drain, do more of the same.

Reframe Rest Guilt

❁

Guilt is a toxin. When the emotion of guilt arises, it often comes from a place of feeling that you don't deserve to focus on yourself. You may feel that it's selfish to be more concerned about your well-being than anyone else's, or that you're neglecting caring about those around you. Guilt about slowing down and focusing on rest in order to heal your body and move forward refreshed has to be gently worked with.

When you experience guilt in resting, you are feeding into the notion that you must drive yourself into the ground to be a person worthy of all that you receive or desire in life. But sometimes you must say no in order to say yes to feeling revitalized and whole rather than rundown and perpetually depleted. Reframe that guilt by looking toward the good—the healing—that comes from choosing rest. Are you more present in your life? Does the world around you seem brighter because you've embraced slowness rather than a harried pace? Are you able to give more of yourself to a goal or to others after rest? Look for these seeds of goodness and plant them wherever the guilt tries to grow.

Build Body Intelligence

Acquiring knowledge is what we are trained to do. Starting with primary schooling, the milestones we reach are lauded with praise to encourage us to keep going. Through enough time of acquiring knowledge, we build intelligence. This extends to intelligence regarding the body. We can look at our bodies and, over years of acquiring knowledge about them, learn to hear and follow the wisdom that they offer us.

Every body is different. Some of us have injuries and physical limitations. Some of us live with chronic pain. Others rarely encounter a body ailment. In being able to sit in presence with our bodies, we can tune in to our own physical abilities and boundaries. We recognize when we are filled, drained, or may need rest. We can also know intuitively when something is wrong and we need to outsource a solution. Pay attention to the little cues—the flutter in your chest, the churning in the pit of your stomach, that back pain that flares. These are all signals of where there is healing to be done.

Heed the Wisdom Within Your Veins

❀

Sometimes we need deeper insight into our bodies—insight that only science can give us. When we want to ensure that our physical healing is on the right track, blood testing can be crucial. *Healthline* suggests getting a full blood work panel—a number of blood tests performed at the same time—at least once a year. This is what most doctors will suggest too. Annual blood testing gives you measurable information about how your body changes over time, especially as you implement your own changes for your physical well-being.

Common blood work tests include a thyroid panel, a complete blood count (CBC), a basic metabolic panel, nutrition tests to check for vitamin deficiencies, enzyme markers if you're predisposed to genetic diseases such as cancer, and sexually transmitted infection testing. The results of these tests can pinpoint disease or problem areas of your health and help you create a plan for healing any new or chronic body ailments. In order to heal, you have to know your starting point.

Trace Your Body Through History

❈

Science teaches us that patterns are inevitable. Very rarely is our individual health solely a matter of the care we extend to our bodies. We are the sum of the countless ancestors who came before us. Our family health history impacts our own. Because of this, we must accept that the predisposition to disease or chronic conditions can be passed down through generations. Asking questions about the health histories of family members can be helpful in the journey to healing.

Part of your exploration will depend on your sex. For example, if your sex is female, you will want to talk to the women in your family about things they have dealt with. Be sure to ask about reproductive health and if certain diagnoses like cervical and breast cancer, polycystic ovary syndrome (PCOS), and endometriosis run in your family. If your sex is male, you will want to ask the men in your family about a history of things such as testicular and prostate cancer. You will also want to take a look at the histories of both sides of your family as a whole for patterns, including heart disease, high blood pressure, high cholesterol, and kidney disease. Ask questions in order to make a more informed plan for your own health and healing.

Create a Healing Vitamin Regimen

❈

Vitamins are elemental in healing and overall wellness. There are limits to what diet alone can do, which is where vitamin supplements come in. They provide the important nutrients you may not eat enough of in your daily meals. If you've done a blood work panel, you'll know which vitamins you generally need to include as a part of your everyday regimen. Vitamin D, vitamin C, and vitamin B_{12} are some common ones.

Multivitamins are one route to take to get multiple or even all the vitamins you may need for your body. Multivitamins include a larger list of individual vitamins in one pill, making them a convenient option. If you'd like a more individualized approach, vitamin subscription services can give you a list of recommended vitamins based on the evaluation form you fill out. Care/of, Ritual, Baze, and Rootine are some subscription options. If swallowing pills is hard for you, look for vitamins that come in capsules or gummy form. Take one at a time versus swallowing them together in a bunch.

Learn about Herbal Medicine

Your local pharmacy is not the only place to find medicine that can help heal your body. Herbal medicine is another route of physical care that focuses on combinations of natural herbs taken orally. Used judiciously, these herbs can provide relief from a countless number of physical ailments and can also help you achieve restful sleep and fluidity and flexibility while moving. Herbal medicine can be an invaluable tool to you as you look for ways to heal your body.

Look toward books and other resources to begin exploring the world of herbal medicine. Organizations like Herban Cura, based in New York City, routinely offer virtual trainings where those interested can explore this modality. The important thing to remember is that you are the student, not the master. Go into it with an open mind and heart, willing to learn and apply that knowledge to your body's specific needs.

Attend Movement Classes

There may be nothing as bonding and mutually beneficial as committing to regular movement within a class setting. Together with your classmates and your instructor, you can experience movement as a community affair, not something you have to explore and go through alone. Having an instructor as a guide also means that if you're experiencing difficulty or are stuck in trying to master a new concept, you can glean their wisdom and find out what works for your body together.

A wide range of movement classes are available, including yoga, Pilates, Zumba, stationary cycling, barre, and high-intensity interval training (HIIT). Because there is a range of activities based on intensity and length, you can choose what works for your body and schedule. By attending classes, you also get the benefit of accountability—both to yourself (especially if you've paid for the class) and to those people you've met in class. This community of others interested in similar activities can be a motivator whenever you experience low morale.

Going to movement classes rather than going it alone means you transition your healing from a solitary endeavor to one with an external support system.

Learn the Basics of Somatic Therapy

❁

Our bodies are complex. One way to build body literacy and body intelligence, guiding us to a higher path of healing, is with somatic therapy. Somatic therapy is concerned with listening to what the body tells us and turning those messages into concrete ways of healing from trauma. It draws a clear connection to how intertwined we are as human beings: Our bodies are not isolated forces, but instead are interwoven into a system comprised of mind, body, and spirit. To take this into account is to take a holistic approach to healing.

To learn more about somatic therapy and how it can impact your healing journey, start by reading about the basics. Research online and look to leaders doing great work in this field. Prentis Hemphill is one great leader in somatic therapy. Their work looks at how body-centered transformation is the key to holistic healing. It also aims to bridge the gap between healing and marginalized individuals who often don't see themselves and their struggles reflected in mainstream healing culture. Consciously and enthusiastically, learn more to heal. Visit www.traumahealing.org or check out *The Politics of Trauma* by Staci K. Haines.

Tap In to Food Creativity

❀

Food is medicine on its own, but it can also be viewed as a way to bring more creativity into your life. Tapping in to your most creative self can be healing, and there is joy and renewal to be found in letting yourself have fun with your life, including with food.

It can be hard to balance external sources telling you what you're doing wrong with your diet and what changes you need to make. Bringing creativity into the process means you lower the stakes and find a way to make dietary choices an exercise in perspective.

Steer away from typical conventions, such as when you should eat certain foods based on the time of day. Follow what feels fun and healing for *your* body. For instance, if you wake up and have a hankering for a colorful salad first thing, who's to say that you have to wait until lunch or dinner? There are no rules, only what feels right for you. Additionally, try adding something new into a dish you make often to shake things up further.

Try Dermal Friction

❀

Dermal friction is an alternative healing modality originating in Chinese medicine. This type of physical therapy involves covering the patient's body in a lubricant—typically, essential oils diluted in a carrier oil—and using a blunt tool to massage areas of tension. The tool used for this therapy is commonly referred to as a gua sha tool. This tool can be used on the upper and lower body, as well as the face. Brisk strokes are used on corresponding acupuncture points. The goal is to improve circulation in the body and to dislodge areas of stress. It can also ease phantom muscle pains, headaches, and fevers.

To try dermal friction, search online for practitioners in your area. Before booking a session, ask questions about how a prospective practitioner approaches this therapy and how often they suggest coming in for sessions. Ensure they are experienced by reviewing their history in the practice and possibly seeking out referrals. As you progress through treatments, watch how lighter and more capable your body feels.

Accept the Physical Impact of Trauma

❈

The body keeps score. Even when we ignore the weight of the hard things we've faced in our lives, our bodies know and they never forget. They remind us regardless of whether we've found the space and courage to wade through what has maimed us in the past.

But in not forgetting, your body offers a radical choice in healing: to face your wounds with honesty, curiosity, and graciousness. In accepting your traumas, you tell your body that you have listened—you have heard its cries and you commit to doing all you can in the present and future to become whole again. You can accept your body trauma by being mindful when triggers pop up and paying them enough attention so that when they emerge again, you can be ready for them. Acceptance and awareness are half of the battle. With both, you have a chance to heal.

Clean Up Your Beauty Regimen

❁

Do you know everything there is to know about the beauty products you use? Are your skincare and body care items clean and cruelty-free? Taking stock of what you currently use and researching to find better options can be yet another step in your quest to own your healing. A lot of beauty products are loaded with toxic chemicals, some of which can lead to disease. Others can be drying or cause inflammation and breakouts. And then there are beauty products that are linked to issues with mental or reproductive health.

Do your research. Search for reviews online from other users, and when in doubt, reach out to the company directly to ask specific questions. Being aware is vital. Everything that you eat, drink, and slather on your skin affects your wellness. Ensure that what you are using to beautify yourself isn't to your harm. Choose clean.

Discern Healing and Harmful Ingredients

❈

Nutrition fact labels impart vital information for using food as a means of healing. A subsection of the label that mustn't be ignored is the ingredients section at the very bottom that lists everything that is in the food. Some of these ingredients have long names that look like multiple words smashed together; many of these are compounds that are used as preservatives to help foods maintain their longer shelf lives in stores. Other ingredients are food dyes that are added to foods to create an appearance that is attractive to the buyer.

Understanding what you're looking at in the ingredients list is as easy as typing it into *Google* while you're grocery shopping. Some ingredients should be avoided completely, like high-fructose corn syrup or Red Dye 40. Both have been proven to cause health issues through prolonged consumption. Other ingredients are okay in moderation or can be beneficial to your health and healing. Knowledge is power; decode food ingredients so you have a firm grasp on what exactly you're eating. If a lot of the foods you routinely eat have harmful ingredients, that's information you can use to make better, more informed choices moving forward.

Call Yourself Beautiful

❄

When you look in the mirror, truly liking who looks back at you is wrapped up in your self-esteem, self-love, and also your physical healing. Our bodies, after all, are the physical reservoirs of our healing. Just as they collect trauma in their muscles, joints, bones, and flesh, they collect the healing work we do for ourselves here too. They work on their own to help heal what hurts us, and can be a powerful ally in our journey to being whole. Of course, being pleased with your appearance can be an uphill struggle for many.

For survivors of trauma, not feeling connected to your body and not seeing it as beautiful is especially common. Your body may have undergone physical changes that can make you feel alien to yourself, especially if there has been wounding, scarring, or your appearance has otherwise been altered.

Start a new practice of thinking of yourself as beautiful by doing some mirror work. Look at your face in the mirror and say out loud, "I am beautiful." You can take this practice a step further by standing in front of the mirror without clothing when you say the phrase. Linger in front of the mirror. Don't rush through saying it. Let whatever emotions arise happen.

Try a Sleep Study

❊

According to *Harvard Health*, the average person spends roughly one-third of their life sleeping. Rest is invigorating—a place where we can allow our bodies and organs to relax and recover. But rest can also be a place of frustration and grief if sleeping does not come easily for you. If you are frequently aggrieved when it comes to your sleep routine, or you never really feel fully rested even when sleeping the proper number of hours, a sleep study might prove helpful.

Sleep studies are typically done at hospitals or independent centers. Those who go to them stay for an extended period of time, overnight at least, so that their sleep can be monitored by professionals. Sleep studies have the ability to unearth sleep disorders like sleep apnea or narcolepsy. With the results in hand, you can create a plan with your doctor to help you go forth into more restful sleep. Some of these plans include tools to make sleeping better, such as a CPAP machine in the case of those diagnosed with sleep apnea or medications for those who struggle with insomnia or an inability to remain asleep.

Eat for Your Body

❊

Bodies need fuel in order to heal and maintain good health. However, every body is different, and thus needs different kinds of fuel. Approach eating based on your unique body and any health diagnoses you may have.

Food recommendations based on your blood type are one method of eating for your body. There are four blood groups: A, B, O, and AB. According to Eastern practice, each blood group requires a certain diet in order for those in that group to feel their best. Eating the diet recommended for your blood group is believed to promote restful sleep and sustained levels of energy.

Another way of eating for your body takes into account the diagnoses you may have received already. For instance, someone who has been diagnosed with high cholesterol needs to eat a diet relatively low in cholesterol to keep those levels in check. Those with diabetes need to eat a diet that focuses on balancing sugar levels. Each diagnosis typically comes with diet recommendations from your doctor. For more detailed insight, consider working with a nutritionist who can create a plan tailored to your needs and lifestyle. Nutritionists are skilled at making the business of eating foods that feel good for you an easy process.

Try Different Food Lifestyles

❁

Eating can be done in countless, creative ways in order to aid the body's healing. Doing so can also feel empowering and encourage more confidence as you take control of your life in a big way.

There are so many food lifestyles and ways of eating to consider. Vegetarian and vegan are some of the more well-known ways of eating, the former being plant-based while the latter is also plant-based but excludes all animal by-products. Some vegetarians and vegans choose this lifestyle simply because it is what their body needs or feels best eating. Others balance that physical need with ethical and moral considerations and values.

A pescatarian diet focuses on mostly plant-based eating but allows for eating seafood. Flexitarian is another lifestyle that offers the flexibility to switch between meat-based and plant-based diets in a routine that is based on how your body feels and what it needs. There are many ways to reimagine the way you eat. Try different food lifestyles to determine what suits you and your unique body.

Rule Out Damaging Habits

❁

How do you feel when you eat? Do certain foods make you feel weird, heavy, or like your sinuses are on fire? While you may have tested negative for food allergies, you may have some food intolerances (less severe reactions) that you're not aware of. Ruling this out through a rolling elimination diet may prove helpful to your healing and wellness.

When practicing an elimination diet, you'll cut entire food groups out of your diet one at a time and wait to see how you feel before slowly adding each thing back in. Before embarking on this diet, check in with your doctor about your concerns and really get in tune with how you feel when eating anything. Does your favorite meal make you feel heavy afterward? Have an itchy or scratchy throat after eating your go-to snack? Are your gastrointestinal problems at a ten after a certain dessert? Write everything down for a few days before starting to eliminate foods from your diet. By taking note of problem foods and slowly eliminating them to see if symptoms lessen, you can take a big step in healing your body.

Drink Your Healing

❖

Getting all the needed nutrients in one day can be daunting. There's the recommended servings of fruits and vegetables for each meal. Then there's the lean protein and carbohydrates and sugars to keep you churning and moving throughout the day. How can one possibly keep track of it all and manage to get it digested when there's so much to do? Drink.

Fresh smoothies and juicing are two routes that you can take to ensure you meet your dietary needs no matter how busy life gets. Smoothies use a combination of frozen and fresh fruit and vegetables blended with a base of ice, cow's milk, or plant-based milk. Smoothies can be sweetened with a little honey or other natural sugar to offset some of the bitterness or tartness some fruits and vegetables produce. Protein powders, peptides, vitamins, and probiotics can also be mixed into smoothies. Smoothie bowls are an option for having smoothies you can eat rather than drink, if that is your preference. Juicing is a lot simpler: All you need is a juicer and fresh produce. Then let the machine do the work. Celery, carrot, and cilantro are three types of juices that are packed with nutrients. You can juice just one vegetable or fruit, or get creative with different ingredient combinations.

Prepare Your Space for Healing

❀

A kitchen needs tools to make it function properly. Cooking consistently and using food as a means of healing physical health is a moot point without having what you need at your disposal to make the dishes you love. If you're new to cooking, review these basics to get you started.

Measuring cups and spoons are essential to ensure you have the right ingredient quantities for different recipes. A toaster or toaster oven is a good appliance for quickly heating up premade meals, cooking frozen ones, and more. Microplanes can shred the hardest of cheeses and give you zest in a pinch. Mixing bowls are great for combining ingredients, tossing salads, or marinating. A can opener allows you to access those cans of beans, coconut milk, tomato sauce, and more.

Last, but certainly not least, you'll need kitchen utensils. This means plastic, rubber, metal, or wooden spoons, spatulas, and tongs for pulling off everything imaginable. Use this list to start outfitting your kitchen with the tools needed to make delicious, healing meals.

Travel the World Through Your Food

❉

The world is a vast place. Sometimes it's not possible to travel to a new environment filled with exciting experiences to be had and memories to be made. But there is an alternative for getting on a plane or boat: the magic to be made in our kitchens. The question then becomes, "Where do you want to go for your healing?"

Take the previous concept of trying a new recipe a step further by learning more about a city, state, province, or country through its food. Turn it into an immersive experience: Find recipes for a snack, entrée, dessert, and drink if you can. Be sure to search for recipes and wisdom from those who belong to the culture in question or are from the city or town that you are "visiting" through food.

Transport yourself to another land. Open yourself to learning more about the world around you. Make eating and cooking fun. And heal in the process as you allow the foods of different cultures to feed your body with their unique, nourishing flavors.

Track the Healing

❁

Diaries are known for being the hallmark of expression. No matter our age or situation, we can take to the pages to share all that we can't bear to keep inside of us. We can let go of what troubles us, work through what confuses or frustrates us, and recognize our progress in life. Translate this strategy to your physical journey by keeping a food diary as a form of noticing and tending to your body's healing.

This isn't about counting calories. This also isn't about being mindful of food for the sole purpose of losing weight. This practice is intended to be a habit and pattern tracker. Perhaps you're not eating enough during the day. Or maybe there's a certain time of day that you allow your healthier habits to fall by the wayside. Maybe you don't get as many leafy greens or fruit as your body would like.

Food diaries are a tool for recognizing those patterns that aren't serving your body and for developing healing habits. A diary is also valuable for digging deeper into food allergies and intolerances, as discussed previously. Use the power of pen and paper to your advantage.

Practice Self-Soothing

❖

As children, we are often taught how to self-soothe when we are overcome with emotion. To self-soothe is to find a place of inner calm and provide for ourselves the comfort we seek from others. (For some, this tool is not nurtured in childhood and must be developed later in life.)

But self-soothing isn't confined to our emotions. We can also practice it to guard ourselves from the intensity of healing our bodies and de-escalate the impact that a trauma may have on us.

When it comes to your physical body, examples of self-soothing include mirroring the physical support that you receive from others. Being hugged while in distress, for instance, can be something you do for yourself. When overwhelmed, sad, or in need of physical reassurance as you endeavor to heal, wrap your arms around yourself and squeeze gently. When more prolonged touch is wanted, self-soothing can take the form of gently rubbing your arm or a reachable part of your back to calm yourself.

Reset Your Body

❖

Most doctors and nutritionists agree that our bodies don't actually need to "detox." Our bodies possess the natural ability to flush and clear out toxicities. We can, however, aid this detoxification and give our bodies a helpful reset following unhealthy habits by intermittent fasting.

Intermittent fasting involves choosing a time period to not eat. The aim of not eating during this time is to make space for more healing by bringing more mindfulness to your everyday life, controlling mindless eating, and perhaps losing weight per the recommendations of your healthcare professionals. Many choose to fast for sixteen hours each day (the 16:8 method), though other popular fasting methods include eating normally five days of the week and eating significantly less for the remaining two days (the 5:2 method) and eating normally for five days of the week and fasting for the remaining two days (the eat-stop-eat method).

An important note: Before embarking on any sort of fast, check in with your doctor. Depending on your current state of health and any medications you may be on, not eating for an extended period of time may not be advisable. Confirm whether this is the best option for you.

Focus On Your Senses

❖

As we grow, we explore and learn more about the world through the five senses. Focusing on sensory processing can be a ripe method for new insights and presence within your body as you self-heal.

Focusing on your senses is more than being present for the physicality of your body. It is about connecting more fully with each sense. When was the last time that you spent your day intentionally engaging in all that sensory knowledge and wisdom your body so freely provides? For example, did you tune in to the smell or touch of your cup of coffee this morning in addition to the taste? Were you conscious of the feel of the ground under your shoes and the sounds of nature or other people around you on your way into the office?

As an entry point to focusing on your five senses, run through this checklist at the start of your day to set an intention:

❏ What one thing can I touch?
❏ What two things can I see?
❏ What three things can I hear?
❏ What four things can I smell?
❏ What five things can I taste?

Consider the Weight of
Collective Trauma

❁

Beyond keeping score of everything we have been through, our body holds the weight of trauma. If you are a member of any marginalized group or community, you know this all too well. Though we may live and breathe, the heaviness of what we survive—and what our ancestors survived before us—is something that exists within each fiber of our being. Discounting the seriousness and weight of trauma passed down from generation to generation is not only insensitive, it is ahistorical.

The truth about self-healing is that you take up the task of healing from not just what you have endured, but also from what those who came before you endured. Retroactive healing has the ability to heal those who have already retired their souls beyond this realm.

Always consider that collective trauma may be a part of the trauma you feel called to heal. If this is true for you, it may make the journey feel harder at times. But in those moments, remember that it is not only an honor to heal but it is a part of your legacy now. Those who came before stand behind you in your journey.

Practice a Walking Meditation

✻

As mentioned earlier in this chapter, there is more than one way to meditate. Just as cooking can be meditative in its own right, so can walking. Taking to the world on foot and letting the breeze blow past you as you reflect can be a personal form of meditation while nourishing your body's need for movement.

To make walking a meditative experience, try taking along the sage guidance of someone else as you stroll around a park, your neighborhood, or any other peaceful place. A quick scan of *YouTube* will uncover a number of guided walking meditations to listen to as inspiration for your own walk. Another option is to use a meditation app like Calm, Headspace, or Insight Timer to follow a meditation for the length of your walk.

Another approach is to start your walk with an intention. This could be through an affirmation that is personally meaningful to you. As you walk, repeat these words while doing some deep breathing. Through any of these methods, walking can be translated to be a healing activity for you, as you release what feels heavy, replacing it with a focus on the present and where your body carries you now.

Adopt a Body-Love Mindset

❖

What is the temperature of how you feel about your body as a whole? Do you hide behind your clothes and other things out of body discomfort? Do you hurl unloving words toward your body on a regular basis? Self-healing requires us to heal our relationship with our bodies into one that is loving, caring, and accepting.

A body-love mindset honors where your body is right now: its physical state, how it appears to you when you look in the mirror, and what size(s) you are. Body-love is not concerned with a future where your body could be different. Your body likely *will* change; it is always working to keep you alive and is in a state of flux as you age and endure. The now, the present, is where your love for your body should reside. After all, the present moment is the only thing that is certain. Why miss out on what you have right here by dwelling on the past or worrying about the future?

One way to walk toward a body-love mindset is to spend time looking at your naked body in the mirror. Look at your body without any barriers. Repeat loving things to your body as you look. Touch your body with the softness of appreciation. There is a path to being in love with your body; take small steps such as this every day.

Deepen Your Body-Love

❊

Body-love, like most things involved in self-healing, is best built steadily over time. Previously, you read about adopting a body-love mindset—that is, embracing your body for where it is right now and not focusing on a belief that your body is yet another thing that needs to be fixed.

As you are right now, as your body is, is good. There is no magical state that you will eventually arrive at that will enable you to accept your body after years of feeling that it wasn't lovable. There is no work to be done to be worthy physically. A caveat: There is a radical difference between saying you'd like to feel more comfortable and safer in your body and becoming fixated on weight loss or body loathing. Many who embark on healing are hoping for some semblance of this.

Deepening your body-love mindset to include these healthy goals for the future involves a few core things such as catching yourself when you say or think unloving things about your body, calling others out when they do the same, and having fitness goals that are about things other than losing weight or dieting.

Check In on Your Stress Levels

❁

Whether it arises from managing the everyday ups and downs of life or the weight of oppression and collective trauma discussed previously, stress is harmful. It can cause your cortisol levels to soar, weighing down your mood and causing body fatigue, an increased risk of heart attack, headaches, and more. Looking at your stress levels and where you can minimize them to allow your body to rest and recharge can be an integral piece of the self-healing puzzle.

When looking at stress and how it impacts your body, start by asking yourself if there is a certain area or areas of your life that are high on your stress list. Second, where you feel stress in your body. For instance, some people get tension headaches or backaches when stressed. Know how stress feels in your body to clue in to when you might be stressed but not consciously processing it.

Once you've asked yourself these questions, dedicate some time to coming up with a few methods for minimizing the stress triggers you've identified and finding healthier coping strategies when you do feel very stressed. Can you delegate or automate a few tasks so you have less on your plate? Could having a standing date for dancing with friends give you a reliable time to release accumulated stress? Get creative.

Seek Alternative Body Modalities

❋

There is more than one way to heal your body. Looking to different healing modalities can breathe new life into the activities that you are employing in the name of self-healing. Some suggested healing modalities for your body include Reiki, cupping, acupuncture, and intentional massage.

Try alternative body healing modalities to discover what feels healing for your body. Take the time to see what's out there and who provides those services in your area. Book appointments with certified practitioners and be sure to ask questions about how you should prepare for the appointment to make the experience a good one.

Last, but certainly not least, focus on enjoying the experience. And if you do not enjoy it, you have one more piece of information to add to your knowledge of what does and doesn't resonate with your body and your healing. There are truly innumerable ways of healing your body and contributing to your holistic health.

Practice Qigong

❁

If it isn't already evident, movement can inspire so much healing on a base level. Through movement, we have the ability to shift stagnant or blocked energy in our bodies, build the muscles that move us from place to place, shake the rust off our joints, and even improve our mood. Our bodies can hold or release our wounds and store lessons, messages, and wisdom available for us to work with if we so choose.

Practicing Qigong, an ancient Chinese method of movement that falls within the umbrella of martial arts, is one way that you can work with your body and the energy force within it. According to *Yoga Journal*, Qigong is best defined as a yoga-adjacent practice. The primary goal is to pair the eyes with the movement of the body in harmony. You can practice Qigong through in-person classes for beginners. Websites like *ClassPass* and *Mindbody* let you search for, sign up for, and pay for classes depending on your location. You can also follow classes or pre-recorded tutorials online through websites like *YouTube*. Start slow to see if Qigong is something you like and is healing for you. Seek community with those who practice it, too, if it does resonate. There is wealth in shared energy and physical body work.

Seek Balance

✻

Beyond the natural foods that fuel our bodies, there are other things that can be digested to help us heal our bodies. However, balance is key, and too much of something can be as harmful as too little of it. Heavy metals are one of these such aids.

Heavy metals like zinc, copper, and magnesium can be taken in capsule form either alone or as part of a multivitamin supplement. In proper doses, heavy metals can help minimize anxiety, lower blood pressure, and improve your heart rate.

Taking too much of any of these heavy metals, however, can be toxic to your body and may require medical intervention. Symptoms like chills, fever, nausea, and gastrointestinal issues can be the result of excess use of heavy metals. If you have questions about what constitutes too much of a specific heavy metal or are experiencing adverse effects, call your primary care physician. Look into working with a nutritionist who is trained to understand individual bodies and can develop a personalized plan to give you the proper fuel you need.

Practice Conscientious Healing

✿

Taking stock of your use of plastic in cooking and storing food can be crucial to physical healing and better health moving forward. Some plastics become toxic when heated beyond a certain temperature.

First, look at your kitchen utensils. Do you have a lot of plastic spatulas and spoons? Clean them properly, removing food and oil thoroughly, and use them as the manufacturer directs. Next, think about whether you store or heat food in plastic. Foods stored in plastic—and especially those heated in plastic—can absorb harmful chemicals. Consider switching to glass containers when heating and storing food. If you'd like to stick to plastic, invest in reusable, nontoxic plastic storage. Though these can be more costly, they are great tools that will put you at ease. In addition, they will reduce waste and can save you money in the long term—not to mention help the environment by limiting waste! What is healing for the earth can be just as healing for you. Of course, be sure to do your research before making a purchase.

Give Your Body the Best Quality

❀

A hot topic in the news and social media, GMOs (genetically modified organisms) can seem like big, scary monsters. But understanding how harmful they can be for your body is an important step in your healing and overall wellness. GMOs are those food items that have been genetically engineered in a lab beyond their naturally occurring state. Certain varieties of corn and potatoes are common examples of GMOs. In many cases, this modification means introducing chemicals and pesticides into the growing, harvest, and/or packaging processes, which can be harmful to your body when ingested.

To remove GMOs from your diet and avoid them in the future, start by researching. Find out common GMOs and how to identify whether something has been modified. Big-box grocery stores are convenient, especially for those in communities that struggle with food insecurity and food apartheid, but there is often not enough regulation of GMOs in these stores. Circumvent this by going local. Find farmers in your area and build relationships with them. Discover smaller stores that sell local products.

If you do shop at a larger grocery store, stick to organic items or the ones labeled as being locally farmed.

Boost Your Nutrition

❀

Fermented foods have been proven to be a tremendous source of nutrients. Health benefits of eating fermented foods include improved gut health and better food digestion. Examples of popular fermented foods include:

* Kombucha
* Kimchi
* Sauerkraut
* Tempeh
* Probiotic yogurt

To incorporate these foods into your diet, seek them out at your local grocer or farmers' market. As noted previously, pay attention to the ingredients label before purchasing a fermented item. Research any unfamiliar items on the label. And be sure to pick options that don't have a ton of sugar in them.

Additionally, you can create your own fermented foods at home. Use Mason jars or other containers to pickle anything you can think of—cucumbers, okra, red onions, carrots, cauliflower. The sky is the limit. Add your favorite spices. Throw in a jalapeño pepper or crushed red pepper flakes for heat. Make it fun! And, of course, make it delicious and nutritious.

Heal Your Gut

✿

Many people don't realize how the body's gut can aid in healing. The gut is the collective of bacteria and fungi that reside within your digestive tract. Healthy amounts of bacteria and fungi facilitate digestion and ensure that your body functions optimally. When your gut health is not the best, however, the bacteria and fungi may be too scarce or too numerous. In either case, thyroid issues, diabetes, and digestive problems are common results.

The easiest way to heal your gut is twofold: First, adjust your diet. Talk to a nutritionist about what is needed to get your diet on track and make a meal plan. Create space to make healthier choices that will in turn make your body feel lighter and energetic instead of heavy and lethargic. Second, take probiotics to balance gut bacteria. Take your time selecting the best probiotic for you before making a purchase. Talk to your doctor about the options available. Start slow, with a smaller amount, and work your way up to an optimal level, depending on your needs. You can absolutely heal your gut.

Learn about the Mouth-Body Connection

❖

Nothing in the human body functions independently. The body is a complex, extremely intelligent system of connected parts. When one part fails to do what it is supposed to, the ramifications are felt elsewhere. This is especially true when talking about healing our bodies and looking at the connections that are underdeveloped and thus impacting us in unfortunate ways.

One key connection that is often overlooked is the body and mouth connection. All those urgings to go to the dentist we've heard throughout our lives weren't just important for our oral hygiene. Our oral health can easily pinpoint issues elsewhere in the body. For example, inflammation and infections in the mouth can travel through the bloodstream to other parts of the body. To take care of and heal our bodies overall, we have to take care of our mouths.

Enact an oral care hygiene routine. Get those annual dentist visits on the books. Select a nontoxic toothpaste brand such as hello or Tom's. Floss on a regular basis.

Firmly and intentionally take care of your mouth to take care of the rest of your body.

Tend to Your Eye Health

❀

The human eyes are the window to the soul. Looking into someone's eyes with intention, you may see their emotional and physical state. For example, weariness may be evident if they are in need of more restful sleep or a reset from stressors. The eyes are also the primary way that many observe and take in the world around them. It is important for them to be functioning well. As you own your self-healing journey, take care of your eyes.

If you wear corrective lenses or contact lenses, have your prescription evaluated annually. Clean your glasses or contacts as recommended. If you don't use corrective eyewear and/or don't often consider your eye health, start with ensuring, like with dentist appointments, that you make an annual appointment with an optometrist.

Beyond regular appointments, take care of your eyes every day. Consider a vitamin supplement that supports eye health, use eye drops to decrease redness, limit screen time to prevent eyestrain, and purchase glasses that filter out blue light for when you do look at a screen for prolonged periods. You should also consider changing your phone or tablet's display to a warmer setting to prevent eye dryness.

Your eyes are precious. Take care of them.

Soothe Your Joints

❁

Walking, sitting, running, sleeping, dancing: All these activities depend on healthy joints. When looking to heal our bodies, paying attention to joint health can be both necessary and deeply illuminating.

Start improving your joint health by moving on a regular basis. Though rest is important, too much idleness and lack of regular movement can create stiffness and pain. Topical balms can also lessen joint pain, especially if you are predisposed to ailments like arthritis. And activities like yoga and Pilates allow you to not only improve flexibility and decrease pain, but also build community with others in a shared interest. This community can help you stay motivated in moving regularly.

Lastly, taking multivitamins made specifically for keeping joint health in line is key. These supplements act as extra insurance for everything else included in your joint health regimen.

Your joints support so much of your body's physicality and ability to move. Why wouldn't you want to take care of them?

Create a Nourishing Skin Routine

✺

Did you know your skin is the largest organ in your body? It is also the glue that holds everything else in your body together. It is crucial to nourish your skin so that you can do something healing, loving, and kind for the body that carries you through life.

To create a nourishing skin routine, first evaluate the current state of your skin and any larger concerns. Do you have persistent eczema that doesn't respond to over-the-counter remedies? See a dermatologist. Are you prone to dry, cracked hands during certain times of the year? Focus on moisturizing more at those times.

Beyond that, look at your daily skin routine. Do you wash your face regularly (at least once per day)? For the rest of your body, do you understand the importance of exfoliation and what products are recommended? Are you layering the moisture you do apply and choosing products that don't contain a lot of fragrance, alcohol, or parabens? Have you tried out different products to find the ones that work well for your skin type and personal needs?

Skin health requires tinkering to figure out what works for you. Take ownership of your skin health.

Better Your Sleep Hygiene

❋

Hygiene is not merely connected to bathing and keeping yourself clean. Hygiene can also be applied to something as important as sleep. And sleep is one of the most healing things you can consistently do for your body.

Sleep hygiene is not about the rest you get. It is concerned with the processes and routines that surround your sleep as well. To create better sleep hygiene, evaluate what could be shifted or improved to help you fall asleep and stay asleep for the recommended number of hours. Maybe you spend a lot of time scrolling on your phone in bed, then find you aren't tired enough to fall asleep. Or you toss and turn because of a noisy mind. Turn off screens at least thirty minutes before bedtime to prepare your mind and body for sleep. Try a sleep meditation to ease you into sleep unburdened from racing thoughts or current stresses. Visit your doctor if better habits do not improve your restful sleep.

Sleep is about regeneration and restoration. As you sleep, your body heals and resets from the previous day. Inject some intention into how you sleep. Create routines that make sleeping a time to look forward to—not one filled with frustration or dread.

Look to Nature

❀

When choosing to spend time in nature, you set the intention to be still and to notice what comes, what falls away, what is pure and beautiful around you. The natural world is the birthplace of humans, as it is of every creature on earth. When dwelling in nature, you return to a place your physical body recognizes as home.

To look to nature as a healing balm for your body, try to do your healing outside and undisturbed as often as you can. Plan a healthy picnic and eat it outside in the sunshine. Take leisurely walks outside to get your movement in for the day. Take a spare five minutes and simply sit on the ground and notice what is going on around you. Lay your yoga mat on the grass instead of doing your asanas indoors. Getting enraptured in nature feels good.

As you heal, as you prioritize your physical health, you deserve to feel connected to and at peace with your body. Nature can give you the chance to experience just that. What a wondrous thing to look forward to.

Envision a Healed Body

✺

Healing is our birthright and yet, when it comes to our bodies, it can feel unattainable at times. This is especially true if your body has become a place of trauma for you—whether an unexpected injury changed your relationship with your body, or you've simply aged and are navigating new pain or conditions. This is natural and a part of what it means to be human.

To build hope and confidence in your healing journey, try the following visualization. First, close your eyes. Breathe in through your nose and slowly and deeply exhale through your mouth. Once you've taken a deep breath in and out, open your eyes and look around. Where do you see yourself in this inner space? Tune in to your body. How does it feel? Now imagine it is radiating with good, positive energy. Run your hands over your body and feel the warmth and that good energy.

Carry this visualization forth as you heal and work toward a body you feel more comfortable and joyous in. You can always return to this space. You can always tune in to your hopes for a brighter, more healed future.

spirit

The spirit speaks if we listen. Like the gentle breeze whistling through tree branches, the spirit can speak in soft tones that guide us to reflect on whether we are living in alignment with our highest truth. Or it can roar like a mighty gust of wind to warn that something just isn't right. When it comes to healing, our spiritual selves beckon to be cultivated.

In this chapter, you'll have the opportunity to deepen current spiritual practices, create new ones, and better understand your spiritual center as a whole. You'll give yourself permission to heal, navigate conflict in your life, look toward your ancestors, and more. Spirit work is sacred work, and so is healing. When the two intertwine, they open up a space for the divine to enter and illuminate what a fulfilling future looks like for you. It's important to work through these activities at a pace that is right for you. There is no rush to healing. Take your time and slowly digest each activity one at a time.

Begin the Journey of Solitude

❀

Learning to enjoy and to look forward to your own company is a gift. In spending precious time alone, you can discover parts of yourself you may have previously ignored. Solitude also gives you the space to listen to yourself without disruptions and distractions. If alone time isn't something you are accustomed to, spending intentional time alone is an adjustment. It may even be scary. What if being alone, embracing solitude, means you get lonely? What if you get bored? These are questions that can arise and are normal to ponder. But being comfortable in solitude has to be embraced in order to heal.

To begin the journey of solitude, accept the gifts found in relishing in your own company. Set the intention to find joy and comfort in spending time solely with the most important person in your life: you.

Learn How to Be a Friend

Friendship is a journey. There are times of connection and times of disconnection. There are moments of intense joy and understanding, as well as moments of frustration and miscommunication. We forge connections with others because the beauty in living—and in healing—is in sharing our hearts with those near and dear. None of us was created to thrive nor survive in isolation. Leaning on others, laughing with others, sharing and becoming vulnerable with others allows us to feel part of something much bigger than ourselves. And through these friendships we gain support. We see that we have people willing to help lighten our load when things get burdensome.

To be a friend, first open your heart. Share a kind word, a hello—anything to open the lines of communication. Then build to more disclosure over time. This is how true vulnerability builds, step by step. Reach out and establish regular patterns of communication, such as a designated time to talk. Suggest an outing or activity during which the two of you can bond. Listen and learn about who your friend is and what makes them unique. Offer insights into yourself in return.

Plan Intentional Solo Activities

❊

As you learned earlier in this chapter, spending time alone can transform your life and aid in your healing. There is so much to be explored and uncovered in your own company. In order for solitude to heal, however, there has to be intention. Bring this intention to your healing journey by planning regular activities to enjoy alone. Depending on how you currently feel about being alone, reorienting your life to view spending time alone as a welcome respite may take some mental reframing. As part of this shift, don't let the planning be cumbersome: Look toward your interests and hobbies, those parts of your life where you allow yourself to be joyful and present in the moment. These are the activities to incorporate into your solo plans.

As with any new habit, it is essential to start slow and build gradually. Planning a solo weekend trip may be a huge leap if you've never looked to time alone as valuable and healing. Instead, start with small pockets of time, say an hour or two, then add more time (and perhaps more distance from home) as you get comfortable. Fill that time with the things you love doing.

Work Through Solitude Discomfort

❈

Solitude can bring up things we'd rather repress and ignore. Things we'd rather not openly and directly confront. As you walk along the path of spending time alone on a regular basis, questions can crop up such as, "Who am I in this world?" and, "Am I spending this life truly existing and acting as the person I want to be? The person who I consider myself to be?" Perhaps you've never dared to ask yourself such huge questions or pondered the meaning of life in this way. Regardless, you may not have clear or immediate answers. That can feel uncomfortable or scary, but remember that not having the answers isn't a bad thing. It means you are considering the possibilities and discovering things as you go. This is how it should be; you are peering into yourself and your place in the world without trying to control what lies beyond the present. Lean into knowing that this feeling of not being settled, of answers not yet known, is temporary. You will not feel like this forever. When the feeling passes, you'll be on the other side of knowing. You'll be able to declare who you are and what your desires are meant for in this life loudly and proudly.

Give Yourself Permission

❄

Through social conditioning, indoctrination, or what was modeled in childhood, we often learn to outsource what we should think or feel, and how to make decisions. This isn't necessarily bad. Existing within a community is powerful. We can lean on others when life is heavy and hard. What begins as insurmountable can suddenly feel survivable when we are not asked to survive it alone. But relying too heavily on community and not enough on our own intuition can dim our ability to discern and thrive.

You don't need the approval of your family to heal. You don't need the approval of your partner to heal. You don't need the approval of friends, colleagues, or neighbors to heal. You don't need anyone outside of yourself to choose what path will allow your trauma to crumble and your wounds to fade. All you need is the decision from yourself. Give yourself permission to light your world ablaze all on your own.

Navigate Conflict

❀

Conflict doesn't feel good. It typically feels uncomfortable and unsafe. Sometimes we even look at conflict as the final nail in the coffin. We assume that disagreeing with someone we care about means the end of that relationship—or that it is doomed to fail in the future. What if you accepted instead that conflict in any relationship is simply a reminder that you are a human in a relationship with someone else equally human?

Each person brings their own "stuff" to a relationship: trauma, wounds, triggers, personal challenges, things they'd rather not relive. We each have our own opinions, perspectives, default reactions, levels of comprehension, and emotional intelligence. When we bring our own stuff to a relationship, tension and miscommunication are guaranteed.

Conflict is not a sign that a relationship needs to end. It is, however, an opportunity for both people to heal if honesty, kindness, and gentleness are the principles we use in communication. Arrive to conflict ready to listen and to find a healthy resolution that feels good for both parties. This is how you heal and deepen your relationships. You can also find helpful insights into your relationship with yourself.

Consider the Impact of Your Physical Environment

❀

A popular refrain asserts, "You cannot heal in the same place where you got sick." The places that bogged us down, that deeply challenged us, that led us to be in need of healing in the first place often are the last places where we can realistically heal and become whole once again. The pain and bad memories only hold us back. When journeying through healing, we have to push ourselves to consider all of what has led us here, especially our physical environment.

Take charge of your healing by exploring whether where you are physically—the city or town where you have chosen to settle or the home where you lay your head at night—could be making it more difficult to heal. Is this the same space where you were first wounded? If this environment isn't primed for healing, make a plan for finding a space where you can better heal.

Talk through what you are thinking with a trusted friend or family member if you want to make a change. Choose someone who can help you process objectively and not project their own opinions onto you. And trust yourself too. You know what you need.

Practice Ho'oponopono

✿

Ho'oponopono, a Hawaiian prayer, is more than popular memes with the words, "I'm sorry, Please forgive me, Thank you, I love you." Hawaiian teacher Morrnah Nalamaku Simeona is credited with first teaching this concept and creating the prayer to distill its meaning. These words are often offered as a first step to bridging the gap between hurt and healing.

When you forgive others—when you take a step on the path of reconciliation after conflict—you are not doing so to absolve those of the harm they have caused. Nor are you saying you pledge to forget that harm as if it never happened. Instead, you are saying that you are committed to your own healing. That you know that hurt and harm take up space and rob you of presence in other areas of your life. You choose instead to free that space without forgetting or dismissing the wounds you have endured. And if you are the one asking for forgiveness, accept through Ho'oponopono that sometimes your words and actions will be too little, too late for the other person. Resolve not to pester them to erase your guilt. Instead, focus on forgiving yourself and moving forward.

Discover Your Spiritual Center

Healing is a long, beautiful, and at times messy ride. Grounding yourself in a spiritual center of calm throughout this journey allows you to find security in intense moments. In your spiritual center you can find safety and resolve when healing brings forth past trauma and emotional muck you'd rather not face. Do you have a spiritual center?

Discover your spiritual center by noticing what you turn to in times of crisis or difficulty. What makes you feel grounded and secure? What gives you peace? Perhaps it's a long bath. Or a meditation focused on peace itself. Once you've identified those grounding rituals, aim to infuse them more firmly into your everyday life. This doesn't have to necessarily be a routine but merely an act of discipline. Rely on them even when life isn't hard. Having the discipline to take care of yourself, to relentlessly tend to your healing, reminds you of your worth and builds the ability to come back to your center when you need it the most.

Ground yourself in this center for reliance when you need to self-soothe, emotionally regulate, and gain clarity.

Introduce Yourself to New People

❊

Making new friends can feel difficult, especially as you age. As you grow older, social circles you encounter are often pre-established. Friends have known each other for years or even decades. They've spent time building their connections through the highs and lows and bonding over shared life circumstances, such as living in the same neighborhood, having kids, or being married. Entering those tight familiarities can feel daunting, but it can be done. And in feeling more connected to those outside of yourself, you will be filling the well of your spirit.

Lead with confidence. Don't give the impression that you are deterred because you are new to those you are trying to befriend. Suggest one-on-one meetings to build individual bonds slowly versus trying to enter into a relationship with multiple new people at once. If you hit it off with one person, the odds are good that you will be introduced to some of their friends too. Lastly, and most important, have faith. View this experience with optimism. Know that edifying connections with those who resonate with you are on the way.

Deepen Established Relationships
with Loved Ones

❖

The connections you have require consistent nurturing. You cannot simply befriend someone and leave things at that. Like the plants that depend on water and sunlight to grow, your friendships require that you tend to them. You have to water them. You have to nurture them, knowing that doing so means you will be nurtured as well.

There are multiple ways of doing this. If you are a busy, overcommitted person, your calendar or to-do lists are probably your salvation. Make notes to check in with friends on a regular basis, whether it's weekly, biweekly, or monthly. The connection doesn't have to take a lot of time—a note to say hello, that you are thinking of them and would love to catch up is sufficient and low stakes. Another way is using technology to automate things more directly: Use a calendar or task app to send you reminders to check in with those in your circle. Tend to your people. Make a choice to do so regularly because you know the power of it.

Create a Personal Holy Place

❁

Place is power. Where we go and where we choose to dwell holds significance for our spirits and can affect our spiritual wellness and healing. Benedictine monk, author, and speaker David Steindl-Rast has written about this extensively. In his book *A Listening Heart: The Spirituality of Sacred Sensuousness*, he writes, "Any place is sacred ground, for it can become a place of encounter with the divine Presence." He goes on to talk about a "personal holy place": a place where the sacred resides within your own effort. To listen to the spirit within and follow its healing wisdom, to make new discoveries that can propel you forward on your life path, find your own personal holy place. Find a place where you feel tuned in to your own soul and the divine around you, and can listen to what they have to say. Nurture that space.

Maybe your personal holy place is a quiet corner in your home. Maybe it's where you go to worship and find fellowship with other believers. Perhaps it's a spot in nature that only you know about. Wherever your personal holy place is, visit it whenever you have a hard moment. Choose to find refuge and insight in this sacred place.

Build Emotional Intelligence

❁

Knowledge from books and the world around you is not the only type of intelligence you can pursue. You can also become well versed in your own emotions. Emotional intelligence involves not only being in tune with what you feel but being able to name those feelings. To be emotionally intelligent is to have the courage to wade through the waves of intense emotion, to be determined to not see feelings as facts or allow them to control you. Emotional intelligence is the first step to communicating effectively with those around you and minimizing or even eradicating the things that cause negative feelings.

To build emotional intelligence, set the intention to honor what you feel and go on the journey of tuning in to and naming what you feel when different emotions show up for you. For instance, if whenever you have to talk to a family member who responds in a volatile manner your stomach lurches and your hands become clammy, you might conclude that you are feeling nervous or anxious. File that insight away to remember when you feel that way again.

Sit with What You Feel

❀

Emotions are volatile, intangible, and automatic. It's no wonder so many of us avoid them. But you can't outrun your feelings forever, and giving them the space to exist is a crucial step in expressing yourself effectively (more on this later). Sitting with what you feel is a companion to building emotional intelligence: You can't understand what you feel if you don't *let* yourself feel.

Imagine sitting across from a dear friend. Your friend is in a state of emotional distress. As they talk, you listen. Listening puts you in the active seat of being a witness to what they feel. That is precisely the point. In listening to your friend share, you are not being tasked with solving anything or fixing their emotional state. You are there to hold space. In doing so, you let them know that they are heard.

Now imagine that friend is you. Imagine the next time when you want to run fast past whatever bubbles up, you instead tune in with curiosity, courage, and earnestness to be a witness to it. Approach it like you would approach the emotions of a friend looking for that listening ear. In doing so, in daring to face what you feel with an unflinching honesty, you start to bind up all the parts of you that are broken, and you begin to heal.

Accept What You Feel
Without Judgment

❁

As you sit with what you feel, judgment may try to rear its critical, hurtful head. The truth is judgmental tones, especially those aimed at ourselves, are too easy. We are, after all, our own worst critics. Being kind in our thoughts and speech requires more deliberation and intent. It means being careful, at times even restrained. Reckless thoughts and speech, on the other hand, enter at will.

When it comes to what you feel, you owe it to yourself to be gentler as you explore your emotions, learn to express them, and heal from them. Be kinder and more precise, acting from a place of measured intent. Don't judge what you feel, even if it is a fury so deep you writhe in rage. Even if it is a sadness so heavy it weighs on your very bones. It is only human to feel these things. Your emotions are not the enemy. They are not to be feared or despised. They are to be seen, held, accepted, and then let go so you can move forward.

Express Your Feelings with Others

❀

Deciding to talk about our emotions can be a huge turning point. For some, this may be uncomfortable or scary. After all, none of us can be sure how others will react when we choose to share our innermost feelings. But in order to grow and heal, and to see our emotions as valued riches of our hearts, we have to learn to express what we feel. In expressing our emotions, we act in alignment with our true selves. And we create opportunities to see the wisdom those emotions can offer.

A good form of modeling is "I feel" statements. Whether sharing a grievance, an observation, or some intense emotion, "I feel" statements allow us to communicate in a way that keeps responsibility off the other person. Sometimes when we share what we feel, we instinctively cast blame or point fingers. "I feel" statements offer another choice—owning what we feel and expressing that in relation to what someone else might have done.

Use "I feel" statements to help you avoid a situation where the other person gets defensive or puts up a wall to avoid being hurt, both of which make communication and resolution challenging. Remember, however, not to become hyperfocused on how you will be received. The response isn't the most important thing here—sharing is.

Ponder Who You Are

✿

Do you know who you are? Do you *really* know who you are beyond what you've been conditioned to believe? Beyond the assumptions you've made without deeper reflection? Questions like these are essential when seeking your own healing. Throughout life, you accumulate baggage, some of which you may not want to lug around: the wounds, the bad memories, and so on.

Questions about who you are according to what you know to be true about yourself is the good stuff. Questions of inquiry are where growth and healing begin. Only when you know what is, can you determine what you want for the future. So settle in. Take a deep breath. Lasso any courage you can find. And ask those questions. Ponder who you are now and how you've grown and changed over the years. If you can, list adjectives to describe yourself. Make the list as long as possible with words that capture who you are.

Release What No Longer Serves Your Spirit

❁

Gut instincts never lie. They know when the usefulness of something has expired or it has no more lessons to offer your life. When what used to be fulfilling becomes frustrating and draining, your gut knows it. It asks you to release these things so that you can make room for all the glorious goodness to come. Release to say yes to your healing and no to what is now deadened energy detracting from your light.

New things can't come in if what you feel lukewarm about, disconnected from, or flat-out uninspired by is taking up valuable space in your spirit. Be judicious in routinely evaluating everything that you lend your energy to, and ask yourself clearly, honestly, and openly whether something needs to remain or be released. When you identify what needs to be cleared, call that thing to mind, whether a material object or ritual, and simply say out loud, "I release you. Thank you for the lessons." Repeat this over and over again as you release to help you fully let go.

Look to Your Ancestors

❈

None of us came into this world without connection. For every human who exists now, there are countless perfect intersections that had to happen in the past in order for them to be created. Imagine that. Consider that. Reflect on that. You are the collision of thousands of choices made in a pattern that will never be repeated again. There is no one like you. And there will never be another person like you. Embrace this as you heal.

Though you may feel alone in your healing, you are not alone. Beyond the tangible bonds that are here in the flesh—the friends and family who care and are ready to lend support—you are protected, cared for, and loved by those who helped to create you. From somewhere beyond this world, your ancestors shower you with wisdom if you're ready and willing to hear it. Call on them. Speak to them. Build an altar if it helps this connection feel more approachable, or simply sit in quiet meditation and speak to them from your heart. Your ancestors want to hear from you and watch you thrive. Lean on them to help you further your healing.

Celebrate Your Friendships

❊

Bonding with friends requires time. And, as you explored previously, a continued, deep connection requires consistent nurturing. In order to fully open your spirit to the restorative powers of these friendships, it is important to recognize the effort you put into them, as well as the healing, fulfilling rewards you—and your friends—reap from these connections. To continue to foster your spiritual healing, celebrate friendship.

Plan a friend gathering somewhere you can relax and enjoy each other's company. This could be in a restaurant, in a wine-tasting room, or an outdoor picnic area. The load may be lessened if the gathering is not your home, because hosting can be quite the investment in terms of time, space, energy, and money.

But if you enjoy the art of planning a menu, cleaning and opening up the sacred space that is your home to friends, then give yourself enough time to plan the details. Let your friends bring desserts or drinks to make them feel like they're sharing in bringing this gathering together through contributing. Keep the guest list low so as to not overwhelm yourself. And lastly, have fun. Enjoy bringing together a group of people whom you care about. Feel the laughter and shared stories fill your soul.

Believe in Miracles

❊

Magic takes undeniable belief. Popular culture portrays miracles as emerging from pain, trauma, and tragic circumstance. For example, the movie or TV show about someone who was in a near-fatal accident but pulled through at the last minute is a common trope. Or the story revolves around someone who did lose their life but was given a second chance. Seeing this played out in media can communicate that miracles are only about being on the brink of disaster.

However, miracles can also be an exercise in faith and seeing things through until you're victorious. Getting there requires digging into your soul and putting a belief out into the universe that the outcome of your healing work will be favorable for you.

Today, tomorrow, next week, forevermore, believe in miracles. Expect them to happen. Expect your healing to be a whirlwind of events and inner shifts that prove that you are enough, that you matter, and that you deserve the world. Because all these things are true. There is no one in the world like you, and that is certainly no mistake. You are a miracle. Believe in more of them to come.

Fill Your Spiritual Well

❀

Scraping the bottom of what is supposed to be a reservoir doesn't feel good. Your spiritual well is meant to be a place of refuge and reliance in difficult times, so it is important to keep it full. Fortunately, even the barest well can be replenished so you can have reserves to heal yourself as well as those around you.

Refilling that spiritual well starts with acknowledging that it is indeed empty. Take a long, hard look at your well and witness where the "water" (the spiritual energy) level is currently. Then go to your spiritual center—that place you explored earlier in this chapter—and draw on its calming energy. Turn to its reminder of safety and grounding as a place to restore your own energy.

Or maybe this is community work. Tap in to your spiritual community. Call on a friend to reassure you that you will be okay and can pour into your well during your time of need.

Hold Space Rather Than
Fix the Problem

❖

Pain is hard to witness, whether the pain is our own or that of people in our social and spiritual communities. We want to be able to *do* something. We want to get rid of that pain. But sometimes the best thing we can do is to hold space, rather than jump into solutions mode. Sometimes what we feel or what we're experiencing simply needs to just…breathe.

Holding space means sitting and listening to someone share (or listen to your own thoughts and feelings surrounding your pain) without giving suggestions or feedback. Reassure them—or yourself—that you see them and see how they feel.

Perhaps holding that space seems too hard, too abstract. Tell yourself—or the other person struggling—that you can hold their "yellow balloon." You can hold that pain without trying to pop, release, or alter it. Solidify this by saying something like, "I know what you are going through is hard. I wish there was something I could do, but there isn't. Instead, I want to tell you that I love you, I'm here for you, and we'll get through this together." Whether to a friend, family member, or yourself, say it out loud.

Listen to the Healed One Within

❀

Sometimes in the throes of healing we are so consumed with changing that we don't see the healing embodied in simply being who we are. But deep within us, there is a sacred dwelling place—a place where the divine, the special, the deep mysteries of the soul reside. And it is possible, with sheer determination and a will to heal, to listen to that voice. To listen to the healed one within yourself.

When you listen to your spirit within, your guidance comes straight from this divine source. The nudges, the silent whispers, all the things that beckon you to change your life are there waiting to be heard. And isn't that mighty relief? Isn't it one less thing to worry about when you count on being saved by yourself and no one else?

Healing is your birthright. You came into this world fresh and new. Somehow through living, you accumulated hurts, pains, and barriers that moved you further from who you truly know yourself to be. It is a difficult truth, but it also means there is healing to be found.

Hone Your Spiritual Identity

❖

Who are you spiritually? Are you a member of a particular religion and look forward to attending services at your local place of worship? Do you instead chart your own spiritual path based on intuitive guidance on what you may need in different seasons of your life? Or is your spirituality simply a matter of relying on yourself to get things done, being confident in your abilities, and trusting your judgment and sense of what is right? There is not one "right" way to own your spiritual identity, but you do need to be clear about what that looks like to you to make it a pillar of your healing. When things get hard, when the healing journey is long, you will want to turn to the spiritual identity you've cemented for validation and comfort. Knowing what your spiritual identity is in the first place is important to that process.

You may already have a few clues to who you are spiritually. Or maybe you have no idea because you haven't pondered it before. It is time to start digging into this question.

Try Automatic Writing

Self-healing can require rigor, honesty, courage, and more. Using words to explore what is coming up for you as you heal can be a valuable insight to motivate you on your quest. This chronicle can also serve as a beautiful map of your journey to look back on once you've entered a different season of your life.

Automatic writing is one way of journaling your experiences, thoughts, and feelings in a more structured way. There are only a few rules for automatic writing: Decide in advance how long you're going to write or how many pages you're going to write, then sit down and write for that time/length without thinking. Do not erase or change what has been written or pause to articulate a thought. Just write.

This type of writing is not intended to be cerebral or emotional. The point is to pick up the subconscious things you may be holding but haven't given any attention to. Look at it as a safe space to unburden yourself on the page. Release what comes up, and don't judge or think your way through it.

Invite In Pleasure

❀

What feels good deep within your spirit? What things or places resonate within you? Pleasure can be a sticky subject. It's something many of us don't let ourselves experience unless we think we've "earned" it. We put off enjoying what feels good because there is work to be done.

But pleasure is as much your birthright as healing and wholeness. You earn it simply by existing. If you invite pleasure in, you can start to see it as a gift ready to give you more of what you need: levity, space for reflection, playfulness, and inner satisfaction. To invite in pleasure, simply ask yourself daily what you can do that would feel good. It doesn't have to involve much thought. What feels good one day might be a quiet moment alone. On another day, it could be an ice cream sundae with plenty of whipped cream, chocolate syrup, and cherries. Don't rob yourself of the chance to feel good. Allow yourself pleasure.

Embrace Your Authentic Self

Unbridled acceptance seems like a tough goal to reach. But embracing who we are simply because we exist and because we are deserving of holistic healing? This is truly a gift to ourselves.

Accepting who we are in spite of our mistakes, blunders, and lapses in judgment can be an uphill battle. We may feel like all our efforts in self-healing are in vain. But it is during those times that we need acceptance the most. It's easy to be confident in who we are when life is good. But when struggles arise, in comes the snap judgments, the pessimism, and the struggle to face our hearts and spirits with kindness and gentleness.

Practice accepting yourself in those difficult moments. Review your list from the Ponder Who You Are activity if it is helpful. Know that as a human you will never be perfect, and waiting on perfection robs you of the chance to love and hold yourself as the unique gift you are now. Lean on this understanding to embrace yourself when it feels hardest, when you want to count yourself out. Know you are worthy, always. As Toni Morrison wrote in her award-winning novel *Beloved*, "You are your best thing." Remember that.

Balance Your Chakras

❋

If you've explored New Age communities before, you've likely heard about chakras. According to Vedic teaching, there are seven chakras total: crown, third eye, throat, heart, solar plexus, sacral, and root. Each aligns with a part of the body, beginning with the crown chakra at the top of the head and ending with the root chakra at the base of the spine. Each chakra also has corresponding themes within healing. The crown chakra relates to higher spiritual guidance, the third eye to intuition, the throat to speech and speaking your truth, the heart to compassion and empathy, the solar plexus to motivation and willpower, the sacral chakra to gut inclinations and inner power, and the root chakra to a sense of groundedness. The chakras are a wellspring of energy within the body, and being able to work with this energy effectively can bring about immense healing.

Balancing your chakras requires both self-inquiry into which chakras are out of alignment and edifying activities to inspire realignment of these energies. For instance, if your throat chakra is unbalanced, you may struggle with asserting yourself to others. To bring balance to the throat chakra, practice small ways of advocating for yourself and speaking honestly, building up to bigger experiences as your comfort level grows.

Find a Spiritual Mentor or Guide

❖

Who guides you? Who can sit with you during spiritually minded tussles and give you spot-on insight? These questions may call to mind a specific person—a friend, colleague, close family member, or trusted sagacious elder. This person, whether you label them as such or not, is a mentor. They are able to walk along with you and instill confidence and a stronger sense of self-worth. As you explore, understand, and hold your healed self, you will need them.

To find a mentor or spiritual guide, approach those who you'd like to be a spiritual companion to you based on a pre-established relationship. Finding mentorship from someone you don't know well can work, too, specifically if you search for people online who present themselves as mentors. Start by identifying what you are looking for—for example, someone with a particular focus such as yoga or energy work—and narrow your search that way. Know in your heart that a spiritual mentor or guide is out there. Find them.

Connect to Trusted Spiritual Communities

❊

Community is everything. Though you may have been brought up on the Western concept of rugged individualism, many cultures around the world believe instead in collectivism—that is, looking to community to lean on in times of need rather than going it alone.

When healing spiritually, you can do both. You can choose what you take on in solitude and when you draw on community support.

Trusted spiritual communities are those that prove to be a safe space for transformation and healing. Do those who surround you make you feel comfortable? Or do they gossip about others or attempt to manipulate your growth in ways that don't feel right? If a community seems negative or bent on your growth looking a specific way, it may not be a safe space for you.

To find a spiritual community, attend social events after services. Exchange contact information with those who present as friendly, open, and interested in you. Just like making friends outside of these spaces, all it takes to find a spiritual community is a little extra effort.

Lovingly Accept Help

❀

There are those we can call on when we are deep in need, those who will be there to aid in our darkest hour. Though self-healing is concerned with the self, others may aid in our journey. And we can accept their help.

You know if you tend to shirk help. Maybe you feel as though you are weak or inadequate if you can't go it alone or push through a challenging situation without any support. Maybe you think self-healing means that you can't ever look outside of yourself. But you can.

Begin opening yourself up to a new realm of possibility by expressing when you need to be supported. Tell a trusted friend or family member that you could use some help and clearly explain what type of aid you are seeking. From there, whoever you have called on will be able to tell you whether they can provide that help. You'll come to find that certain people will consistently be at your aid whenever asked. Turn to them—accept their help with gratitude.

Learn about Human Design

❀

A mix of astrology, the chakra system, I Ching, quantum physics, and kabbalah, Human Design is a means of unlocking spiritual understanding that can facilitate deeper self-healing. Consider Human Design to be a manual that can lead you to more self-mastery in all aspects of life.

Discovering your unique Human Design chart, called a BodyGraph, is as simple as entering your birthplace, birth date, and birth time into any number of websites dedicated to this tool.

A few Human Design basics to bring with you as you find and interpret your chart: Everyone has a "strategy" that is either Manifestor, Manifesting Generator, Generator, Projector, or Reflector. Everyone also has an "authority" that is either ego, lunar cycle, sacral, emotional, or splenic. When Human Design is used effectively, you pay heed to both your strategy and authority in order to make decisions for yourself that are aligned with your needs (both in general and for healing), your personality, and your tendencies.

For deeper insight into how Human Design can help with spiritual healing, look to Human Design experts Aycee Brown and Camille Telicia. Both can be found on *Instagram*.

Pull a Daily Tarot Card

❋

Tarot is also often misunderstood. It is not fortune-telling. A card will not suggest that someone you love will die, your beloved romantic relationship will end, or your life will come crumbling down piece by piece. Tarot, above anything, is intuitive guidance—spiritual guidance. There is no inherently "bad" card or one correct way to read a card. The wisdom of each card you draw is rooted in your personal experiences, needs, and desires.

In order to harness this powerful guidance, get in the habit of pulling a tarot card every day. After you pull your card for the day, take some time to sit with what you think the card suggests for you and your life. Keep that wisdom with you as you carry on throughout your day.

A helpful way to chronicle your daily card pulls is to keep a tarot journal. At the same time that you buy a tarot deck, buy a journal and a nice pen. Each time you pull a card, write down the card you pulled and reflect on what spiritual messages the card is trying to impart to you. Over time, you'll start to see patterns with your pulls. Enjoy the journey.

Plan an Inner Child Date

✤

In Chapter 1, you learned that healing can be found in reparenting yourself. In reaching back to get to know the child within and teaching and giving your younger self the things they didn't receive previously, you allow a greater connection to all the parts of you. Not only is reparenting key to healing your mind, it is also key to healing your heart and soul. That child and the wounds and wisdom they carry exist not just in your thoughts, but also in the core of your being.

Take the reparenting to a deeper level by planning an inner child date. The idea is to create dedicated time and space to commune with your inner child. Make this time fun. What would be enjoyable for you? Some examples include dressing up, blowing bubbles, and playing hopscotch. Create an itinerary for the day. And tell those who might be expecting you to be available that you will not be free during that time.

This time is for you. Honor that it is yours and yours alone to relish. Plan to do an inner child date once every four months or so. Work your way up to a greater frequency depending on the relationship you begin to foster with your inner child. As it deepens, you'll want to spend more time together.

Craft a Healing Morning Routine

❖

How you start your day, whether with intention, apathy, or a haggard mad dash to finish all your responsibilities, sets the tone for the entire day ahead. There are twenty-four hours given to us each day. In order to use them wisely and get as much joy and healing as we can from them, we must employ structure and intent.

Routines can have a grounding effect, minimizing difficulties and giving us something to look forward to. When our spirit is in need of nourishing, when healing feels heaviest, we lean into our routine as something we can count on.

To create a healing morning routine, make a list of what you need to feel energized throughout your day. In terms of energy for the physical body, this could include a healthy meal, vitamins or other medications, and/or a warm beverage such as coffee or tea. In terms of energy for the spirit, this could include a meditation, prayer, and/or energy work you perform on yourself.

Routines are what we rely on. They also create an all-abiding sense of self-trust because you know that you can depend on yourself in that routine. And dependability is life force as you heal.

Create Safe Zones

✿

We live in a cluttered, busy, distracting, and overstimulated world. The world does not encourage us to listen to ourselves, to slow down enough so we can hear and take in the wisdom sorely needed. In order for us to find the refuge that we need to tune in to ourselves and our spirits, we must make a concerted effort in the name of our healing—an effort to seek out safe spaces.

Clinical psychologist and author Dr. Ramani Durvasula has golden insight on this very subject. According to her, technology and social media can be rife with those who invalidate the truths of others, leading to unsafe interactions. To feel safe in being ourselves and discovering our truths, we must create safe spaces.

To create these "safe zones," as Dr. Durvasula calls them, identify those people you feel safest with—those you can count on to mirror your realities back to you, who listen, who validate your truths, and who make you feel accepted rather than rejected. The safe zones created when being with these people are vital to healing. We need to feel safe to unpack our wounds. Go where you are loved and heard.

Turn to Energy Work

❀

The very first law of thermodynamics, the Law of Conservation of Energy, asserts that energy can neither be created nor destroyed—it can only be transformed from one varying form to another. When it comes to spiritual self-healing, this is good news. The energy that constantly flows through each of us can be altered wherever it may be stagnant or overwhelming.

One way to work with your energy is through Reiki. Reiki is a Japanese form of energy healing. Practitioners offer their clients a combination of traditional massage methods and specific hand movements designed to facilitate healing within their bodies and spiritual centers.

Another way to work with your energy is through cupping. Also a form of Eastern alternative medicine, cupping uses small glass cups suctioned onto pressure points along the client's back to improve blood flow, ease pain, and promote relaxation.

Search for practitioners of Reiki, cupping, or other kinds of energy work in your area. Read reviews carefully. Look through their offers to see which professional and modality would meet your needs. Hydrate before any session.

Build a Spiritual Contemplation Practice

❀

When approaching self-healing, contemplating spiritual truths, revelations, and the new healing that has emerged is crucial. This introspection is how you tap in to your soul and understand your spiritual power.

Start small. Ask yourself where in your daily life you have a spare five minutes to simply witness what is coming up for you spiritually without judgment. Invest in that contemplative space without hesitation. Over practice, increase your contemplation to ten minutes, then fifteen, and so on. Build to a time frame that feels personally fitting.

Once you've got the time down, consider adding more things into this practice. Perhaps start your contemplative practice with meditation or by doing Reiki on yourself. Or combine your contemplative time with drinking tea or eating a special meal. Pairing contemplation with other everyday activities is a way of making it more concrete and signaling to yourself that it is an integrated part of your life.

There are no rules when crafting healing practices that are geared to you. The only real measuring stick is whether it resonates with you.

Create a Custom Prayer

❁

If occupying religious or spiritual communities is not new to you, you know about those eloquent petitions to a higher being. Prayer, however, can extend beyond established words in a place of worship. It can be a personalized message tied directly to your own spirit, leaning into your own healing. It can be an invitation, an ongoing monologue, conversation, or witnessing.

Prayer is not about off-loading a long list of requests to an omnipotent being. Prayer is about being present. It is about showing up to life and having faith that you will be shown the way forward. And it is about knowing that healing is on the way, even when it feels far from where you stand.

To create a custom prayer, open your heart. Share what is in it—what it is yearning for and what it holds to be true—and trust that you will be heard. Write down things you'd like to say if it is helpful. Take creative liberties where you see fit.

Join a Prayer Circle

❀

There is strength in numbers. When many people gather to share and open up their hearts, the healing is amplified tenfold. That type of power is what you may need as you journey to healing and spiritual wholeness.

Join a prayer circle through the spiritual communities you explored earlier in this chapter. If you have yet to join a community, recognize that you don't necessarily need to meet with your prayer circle in person. You can find these groups via websites such as *Meetup* by searching for prayer circles in your local area. Additionally, you can seek out these connections through *Facebook* groups that meet over live video or through a conference call.

Prayer is an uplifting force. In prayer, you unleash the power of radical listening and radical witnessing. Take these steps to find the prayer circle that feels edifying and nurturing for you.

Find Time for You

❃

When was the last time you dedicated a day just to yourself? Earlier in this chapter, you explored solitude. You practiced embracing it to make the space needed to be what you want—and discover more about who that true you is. You uncovered how solitude can be healing if you choose to look at it that way.

Beyond simply being alone and enjoying time with yourself, however, put effort into deepening your spiritual practice. Practicing spiritual witnessing, creating a channel of communication with your ancestors, and finding your spiritual center are vital. But you cannot pursue this healing if you do not prioritize time for yourself.

Find uninterrupted time for you today. Clear your schedule for a few minutes, a few hours, or even the whole day. Slip away to a quiet space in your house or go somewhere secluded in nature. Once you're in your quiet space, do whatever feels fulfilling for your spirit. You'll find as you become more intentional, pockets of time will present themselves regularly for your healing.

See the Gratitude

❁

Gratitude is an inside job—one that has to be cultivated in order for it to grow. A number of holidays across the world focus on this through the gathering of loved ones, breaking bread together, and sharing the things they are grateful for. It is about naming gratitude to widen the spectrum of awareness.

See the gratitude in your own life through calling to mind the things that you may often overlook: a cloudless sunny day, a blooming flower, laughter in the middle of a hard day. Try putting this into practice by using a gratitude journal. Start or end your day by writing down a few things you are grateful for. A gratitude journal allows you to not only call awareness to what is good in your life but also return to those things when you are feeling negative.

Let the universe and your own spirit know you are listening and paying attention to the wonderful things in life. Practice recognizing what you have, and more of the same may come your way as you continue to heal.

Let Love In

❀

When the Beatles released their ever-popular song declaring that "all you need is love," they were onto something very true. Love can be precisely the healing balm that you need as your walk toward spiritual healing and wholeness. Love is a spiritual force. It binds up wounds and lightens the weight of healing work.

This is not a declaration for only romantic love. There are all kinds of love to be given and received to heal your soul: love for and from friends, family, pets, and so on.

Letting love in is as simple as saying out loud, "I will let love come into my life with an open heart," and proceeding with that intention. Another method is telling the people in your life that you'd like to work on better accepting and giving love. Share with them what you need in order to feel loved. It could be as simple as physical affection or being told you are loved. It could be sharing what your love language (one of five types of giving and receiving love, discernable by taking a simple quiz online at www.5lovelanguages.com) is so those in your life can discern how to show up for you—and asking others what they need in order to be loved too.

Witness Synchronicities

❁

Everything within the realm of this universe has its place. Though sometimes the things that happen in life are random and disordered, other times we can see clear patterns in what occurs. Our healing and lives as a whole are shown to be intentional, and lessons and wisdom are imparted to us.

Sometimes the things that unfold in those patterns are synchronicities—things that feel related but cannot be explained by science. It is up to you to discern what wisdom or important information can be found in these synchronicities to foster more spiritual healing.

To witness synchronicities, draw awareness to how your life has unfolded. Was there a certain event that seemed to fall into place too perfectly? Did something that you'd been planning fall apart at the last minute, then later prove to have a terrible outcome you were able to avoid? Journal and reflect on these questions. The goal here is to cultivate awareness of synchronicities. Once you begin to notice them, you can work to interpret what they may be telling you about your spiritual alignment—whether you are on a path true to your spirit or not. Choosing to see synchronicities provides a chance to own your healing and widen the sphere of your spiritual life.

Release Low Vibrational Things

❉

Part of any kind of healing is letting go of what burdens you. As you heal your spiritual self, surround yourself with things that will inspire you to new heights. Low vibrational things (materials, activities, places, etc.) are the things that do not resonate with you on a higher spiritual level and are an important place to begin releasing what is unhelpful or not motivational to you.

The main way to know whether or not you are clinging to low vibrational things is to ask yourself if you feel in spiritual alignment. Take an honest look at your life as it is right now: Do you spend a lot of time embroiled in things that don't bring you joy? Are there a lot of things in your life that don't lead to healing or growth? Or even make it more difficult to heal or grow? If you answered yes to any of these questions, it may be time to release those things and make space for what could be more in alignment with you and the spiritual healing you seek.

Ready Yourself for an Awakening

❖

Often you'll see clear signs that you are being ushered into a new season of spiritual life. When it comes to healing, these seasons of "initiation" can be marked by loss, confusion, grief, and a release of many things in your life.

Some of these signs are detachment from what once felt like home to you but may no longer be helpful or a source of joy. You may find yourself experiencing a restlessness in parts of your life, a drive to reevaluate your spiritual core beliefs, your place in a spiritual community, and more. This stirring is proof that as you are being called to heal, you will need to shed some things before you can move into a new level of your life.

To ready yourself for this awakening that happens in tandem with spiritual healing, check in on your spiritual self-care. What are your routines for fostering groundedness? Simple grounding techniques include walking barefoot on grass and wrapping your arms around a tree. Once you've evaluated your self-care and added or altered anything to help you better ground yourself, reassure yourself that though this current phase may feel scary and unfamiliar, it's for your good. On the other side, there will be a healed you aligned with your true spiritual identity.

Take Stock of Your Relationships

❊

Building on the previous activity for readying yourself for a spiritual awakening, it's also wise and prudent to take stock of all the relationships you've accumulated. Are they taking you to new heights, or weighing you down with baggage from the past?

Relationships and community are extremely important. In this chapter, you have explored spaces dedicated to fostering new connections and finding like-minded people for spiritual sharing and growth. But sometimes people overstay the period of time they are meant to be in your life. Sometimes a relationship shifts from helpful to harmful. Or you simply outgrow it.

Start practicing the sacred release of all that does not serve you by taking honest inventory of all your relationships—new and old, close and not so close. Notice whether or not the dynamic fostered still feels good to your spirit. Do you walk away from interactions feeling drained or uplifted? If it's the former, it may be a sign that this person no longer resonates with you.

This is okay. Letting relationships go doesn't mean you or the other person failed. Quite the contrary; they have completed their purpose. Let them go with love, reverence, and gratitude.

Practice Tapping

❖

There are many ways of tending to the spiritual overwhelm that may arise as you heal, ways that can encourage spiritual growth. One of these is the Emotional Freedom Technique, also known as EFT or tapping. EFT uses a method of tapping certain points on the body to balance energy and reduce pain.

To tap, find a quiet place. Start taking deep breaths and invite what is causing you anxiety into this place with you. With your right hand, tap each finger on your left hand a couple of times, beginning with your thumb. Take your time doing this. Continue taking deep breaths as you tap. Switch over to the other hand and repeat the process.

As your heart rate slows, notice your breathing become deeper. When you feel ready to stop, gently shake out your hands and express gratitude for this practice.

Return to tapping whenever you feel overwhelmed. You can also tap other parts of your body in addition to or instead of your hands. The feeling of being overwhelmed lives in the spirit. It can rob you of your intentional presence. Tap to step back from it and see the bigger picture.

Use Crystals to Spiritually Ground Yourself

More than pretty things to look at, crystals can be an incredible tool for practicing spiritually grounding in order to address healing with confidence and clarity.

Begin your experience with crystals by finding a metaphysical store near you. You can, of course, purchase crystals online, but with crystals it's super important to let them speak to you. Let the ones you are meant to have literally call out to you as you browse. This is much easier done in person.

Once you've purchased your crystals, take them home and put them in a designated place. You can place them on a nightstand or put them in a drawer or container. You can also carry them with you in an everyday tote or turn them into jewelry you can wear regularly.

To tap in to their power, let your crystals charge under the new moon by simply placing them on a window or table ledge, open porch, or anywhere else where the light of the moon can shine down onto them. The energy from the new moon is said to infuse your crystals with more potency to aid in your spiritual healing. Once charged, you can use their power by placing them underneath your pillow, in a bag you carry with you each day, or in your car.

Smudge Your Space

❀

More than a popular activity for New Age followers on social media, smudging is an age-old art that has its roots in indigenous communities across the North American continent. The aim of smudging is to clear deadened energy and lighten up spaces that may feel off energetically. Smudging is most often done with bundles of dried sage and/or palo santo.

To experience how this spiritual clearing practice can aid in both healing and transformation in the physical spaces you occupy, find ethical places to purchase sage, palo santo, or another smudging herb bundle of your choice. Refrain from buying an herb bundle online unless you can verify where it is ethically sourced.

Once you've purchased your smudging bundle, light one end. When it has caught flame, blow it out and let the smoke rise from the burned end. Speak intentions out loud of what you'd like to bring to your space as you touch the smoke to each corner of the room. Open the windows as well so any leftover negative or stagnant energy can escape. Express gratitude for this practice at the conclusion. Store your smudging materials for whenever you may need them in the future.

Travel to Sacred Spaces

❀

Sometimes we are called to stay still and invite in the spiritual guidance that is knocking on our door. Other times, we are called to move, to experience the world more so we can encounter insights and lessons that nourish our spiritual spheres. The act of travel can not only be exhilarating, but it can also provide new perspective and aid in spiritual healing.

Turn travel into a spiritual activity with healing in mind by traveling to sacred spaces. There are many around the world that are gathering places for those seeking to find spiritual refuge. The Holy Island of Lindisfarne is one example. A low-tide island, it is believed to have once been a monastic community in England. Today, the area acts as a special place to be spiritually refilled and inspired. Another example is Sedona, Arizona. The characteristic red rocks and awe-inspiring sunsets and sunrises are what this area is known for. But it is also known for being an energy vortex where people can come to accelerate spiritual healing.

Use travel to see more of yourself and invite healing into your soul.

Create New Spiritual Rituals

❁

Rituals fill us up and remind us of who we are. When it comes to spiritual healing, rituals of spirit can round out a good day and bring us out of the depths of a bad one. Creating new spiritual rituals can be a great way to usher in new or revitalized healing.

To develop new rituals, look to the season of weather you are in for inspiration. The seasons represent the phases of life and serve as powerful metaphors for the spiritual self. Use these themes to hone a healing ritual of your own. For example, if it's winter, can you do something in honor of hibernating and expectancy for what will bloom in the warmer months? If it's fall, can you practice shedding what has ended or no longer serves you in order to create a mindset that is ready to be more still and quiet in the coming winter?

Take different options depending on these considerations. There are ways to center your spiritual healing that bring new life to your practices. The patterns of life inspire you to do just that. Because as you heal, you are allowed to find joy in the process.

Center Your Spirit in the Present

❖

Escapism is a tactic used when we can't bear to remain in the place where the pain, heaviness, and harsh realities of healing our spiritual selves resides. To escape it all, we run. We distract ourselves from our calling to heal. It is easier, we tell ourselves, to hide. Perhaps, we think, it will go away if we avoid it long enough. But the truth is that this calling will never go away—never stop chasing us—until we find the courage and fierceness to face the resolve to turn and embrace our lives with *all* that it may come with.

Notice when you are trying to distract or numb yourself, when you employ those personal habits cloaked in avoidance. And when you catch yourself, breathe deeply and sit with what has arisen for you spiritually. In being present, you may experience a heavy weight in the pain and emotions you are facing. But do not turn and run. This is where spiritual self-soothing comes in to carry you through that weight. Praying, reaching out to a friend, pulling a tarot or oracle card, and any other spiritual grounding and healing exercises can help exalt you beyond the pain.

Mark Your Spiritual
Healing Birthday

❊

Birthdays are special times of year. From a young age, it is communicated to us what a celebration it is to live another year. And really, it is a wonder to be alive. Life is fleeting, and not one moment is guaranteed. It makes sense that birthdays can take on such special meaning.

Birthdays don't have to solely mark another year of life, however. You can use them to celebrate your spiritual healing and the growth and lessons accrued from the start of this journey. You can choose to recognize and mark how far you've come. Beyond appreciating the work you have put in to come this far, marking the occasion can help motivate you to continue on your journey no matter what may come.

Reflect back on when you first set out on your journey to heal. If you can't quite remember, flip back to your journal or ask those in your spiritual community. Perhaps they will recall. When you identify the date, plan a celebration to mark it. Eat your favorite dinner. Watch a favorite movie. Have a delicious dessert. Whatever you do, celebrate. Each year, when this date comes back around, treat it as a special day that ushered you into a new chapter of healing.

Identify Your Spiritual Medicine

❖

When we are sick, we know that the first step is to go to the doctor. We lean on the understanding and expertise of the doctor to help us get well. Medicine is a part of this healing. With a prescribed combination of methods, we are nursed back to health.

Consider spiritual healing as a course of action similar to this: You are in need of "medicine" that will mend your wounded soul and help it feel whole and thriving. Consider it a spiritual prescription; what is in yours? Write down what you need for healing. Maybe it's a combination of being in a spiritual community, praying, and connecting with trusted friends. Perhaps it's energy work and meditation. Whatever helps you align with your spirit and its truths, and fills you up in healing, joyous ways, write it down. If you aren't sure what your spiritual medicine is, use the earlier activities in this chapter to explore and find out what it may be. Then give yourself the medicine you need so you can be well and heal.

Start Anew

❊

As clichéd as the saying is, the longest, most winding journeys do begin with one step. One decision. When you set out to heal, you don't know where you will land. And it's no consolation knowing that the process will be filled with challenges as you face your shadows and learn how to let them go with grace.

Starting over, as scary as it may seem, is an exercise in courage. A fierceness resides in the spirits of those who set out on an unknown path with hope that it will bring them something different that they need. Over the course of history and storytelling, the hero's journey has proven exactly this.

If you feel out of alignment with your healing goals, it may be time to find your courage within and start on a more edifying path. It may be time to reset your spiritual space for new lessons and healing and put aside what no longer works. Say goodbye to those things with the utmost amount of love and gratitude. Accept that you are venturing somewhere new. Then forge onward with the conviction that all will be okay. Your spirit certainly knows this to be true.

about the author

Nneka M. Okona is a freelance journalist who has written about self-care, wellness, and grief for *Well+Good*, *MindBodyGreen*, *The Washington Post*, Headspace, and *Yahoo Life*, among many others. A budding tarot enthusiast, forever wandering spirit, lover of hours-long cooking projects, and aspiring yin yogi, Nneka lives in Atlanta.